The Positive Behaviour HANDBOOK

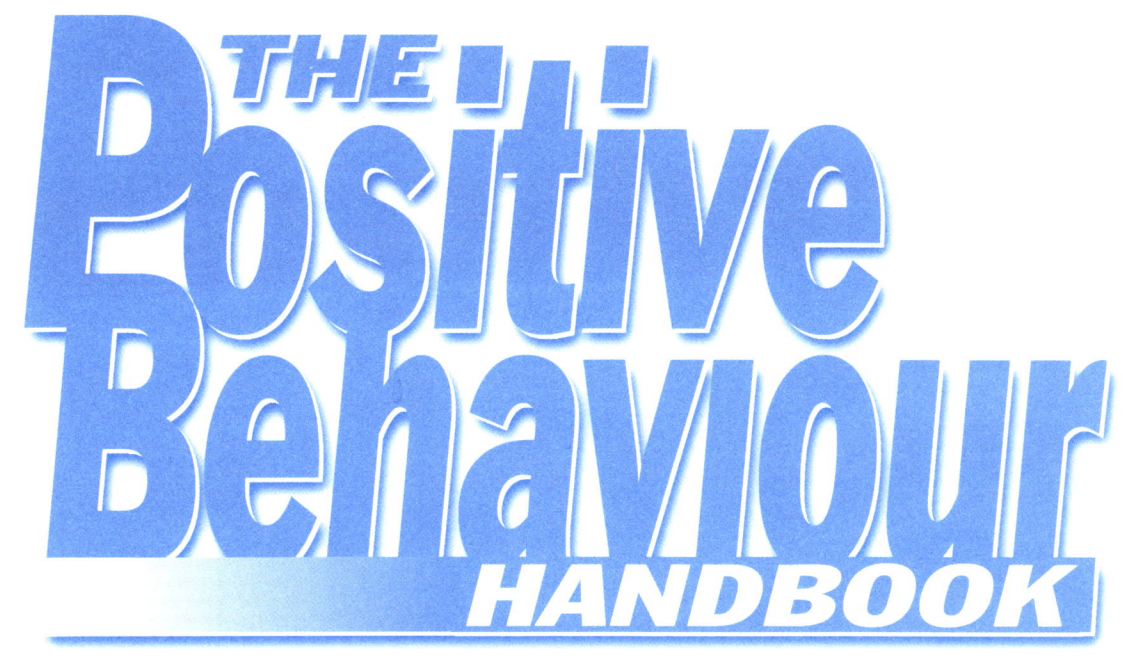

The complete guide to promoting positive behaviour in your school

Lynn Cousins • Julie Jennings

pfp

pfp publishing limited

© pfp publishing limited 2003

First published in Britain in 2003 by
pfp publishing limited
61 Gray's Inn Road
London WC1X 8TH

Writers Lynn Cousins, Julie Jennings

Design Martin Harris Creative Media

Photography Corbis, Photodisc, Nicholas James

With special thanks to Oldway Primary School, Paignton, Ilsham C of E Primary School, Torquay, Collaton St Mary C of E School, Paignton

Printed and bound in the UK.

A catalogue record for this book is available from the British Library.

All rights reserved. No part of this publication may be reproduced, stored in a retrieval system, copied or transmitted without written permission from the publisher except that the materials may be photocopied for use within the purchasing institution only.

ISBN 1 874050 71 6

pfp orders and customer services
FREEPOST 59
Rochester ME2 4BR

Tel: 0870 241 0731 Fax: 0870 241 2765
www.pfp-publishing.com

CONTENTS

Introduction	4
1 Skills for teachers	6
Starting the year off well	7
Day one: rules and routines	13
Circletime	17
Talking to children	21
2 Involving the children	25
Developing high self-esteem and learning about criticism	26
Taking responsibility	37
3 Rewards, sanctions and expectations	43
Rewards	44
Sanctions	51
4 Involving and supporting parents	54
Writing to parents	55
Parents' evenings	61
Writing reports	63
When parents help in your classroom	65
Parent workshops	67
Workshop 1	70
Workshop 2	75
Workshop 3	79

Introduction

PROMOTING POSITIVE BEHAVIOUR through the development of children's emotional health and wellbeing in the classroom situation

In our schools there are many children who behave well, who listen, concentrate and learn, children who treat others with respect and are happy to be in class. Their behaviour can be described as **positive**.

The children who receive most notoriety in the media are those who play truant, and who are aggressive and disruptive when in class. Their behaviour can be described as **negative** or **unacceptable**.

In between is a layer of **acceptable** behaviour. Often it is only to this level that we raise the negative behaviour – so we have children who may not be aggressive or disruptive, but who may not yet have reached the level of positive.

The ideas and advice in this book are intended to raise the level of behaviour beyond acceptable to positive. We suggest ways to promote the positive behaviour already displayed by many of our children, to recognise their efforts and to draw attention to the contribution they make to the wellbeing of the class, so that this behaviour becomes the norm and not the exception. There is advice on how to respond to those children who are now behaving at an acceptable level so that they can continue to strive to reach the positive. There are ideas for you to use to start things off in a positive manner and keep on top of the behaviour of your class.

What do we want our children to be?

- Respected.
- Respectful.
- Secure.
- Helpful.
- Loved.
- Caring.
- Sympathetic.
- Stimulated.
- Adaptive.
- Inquisitive.

How would we recognise these qualities?

- **Respected** – other children ask his advice or approach him for help.
- **Respectful** – he is always polite to other people – adults, children, visitors.
- **Secure** – if he gets something wrong in his work he can accept comment as supportive criticism and try again.
- **Helpful** – he notices and reacts to situations in the classroom and will tidy away or set the books straight without being prompted.
- **Loved** – he comes into school with a smile on his face and is positive in his attitude to life.
- **Caring** – he sees another child hurt on the playground and goes to his aid.
- **Sympathetic** – he sees another child drop a tray of pencils and goes to help him pick them up.
- **Stimulated** – he is keen to take part in classroom activities, eager to learn and have a go at new challenges.
- **Adaptive** – will work equally well for a supply teacher and isn't upset by having a new teacher.
- **Inquisitive** – when he finishes an activity he will go and find something else to do, a book to read or extend the activity and set his own challenge.

The child is the product, sometimes even the victim, of his own circumstances. It is the skill of the adults in the school, and their emotional maturity and stability, that will enable him to overcome any negative influences and give him the self-respect he needs and deserves. Figure 1 illustrates this.

Behaviour is the interplay of the child's emotional state (the passive) with the child's physical reactions (the active). Each is continually reacting to and influencing the other. We can see the child's actions, but may have to search for the truth of the child's emotional state.

As teachers we deliberately affect the child's active side – 'sit still', 'speak up', 'don't snatch'. Our effect on the passive side is more subtle; it is often unplanned and unintentional, but it is a constant presence and is a major influence on the way children behave.

Children who have self-respect and a high level of self-esteem can face adverse circumstances with a degree of equanimity. They can stand up to the potential bully without becoming a victim. They have no need to treat others in negative ways and are unlikely to become bullies themselves.

Children who feel secure and respected can take full advantage of the learning opportunities we provide for them. They are adaptive and inquisitive. They are able to learn from their mistakes and use all the experiences in their lives in positive ways.

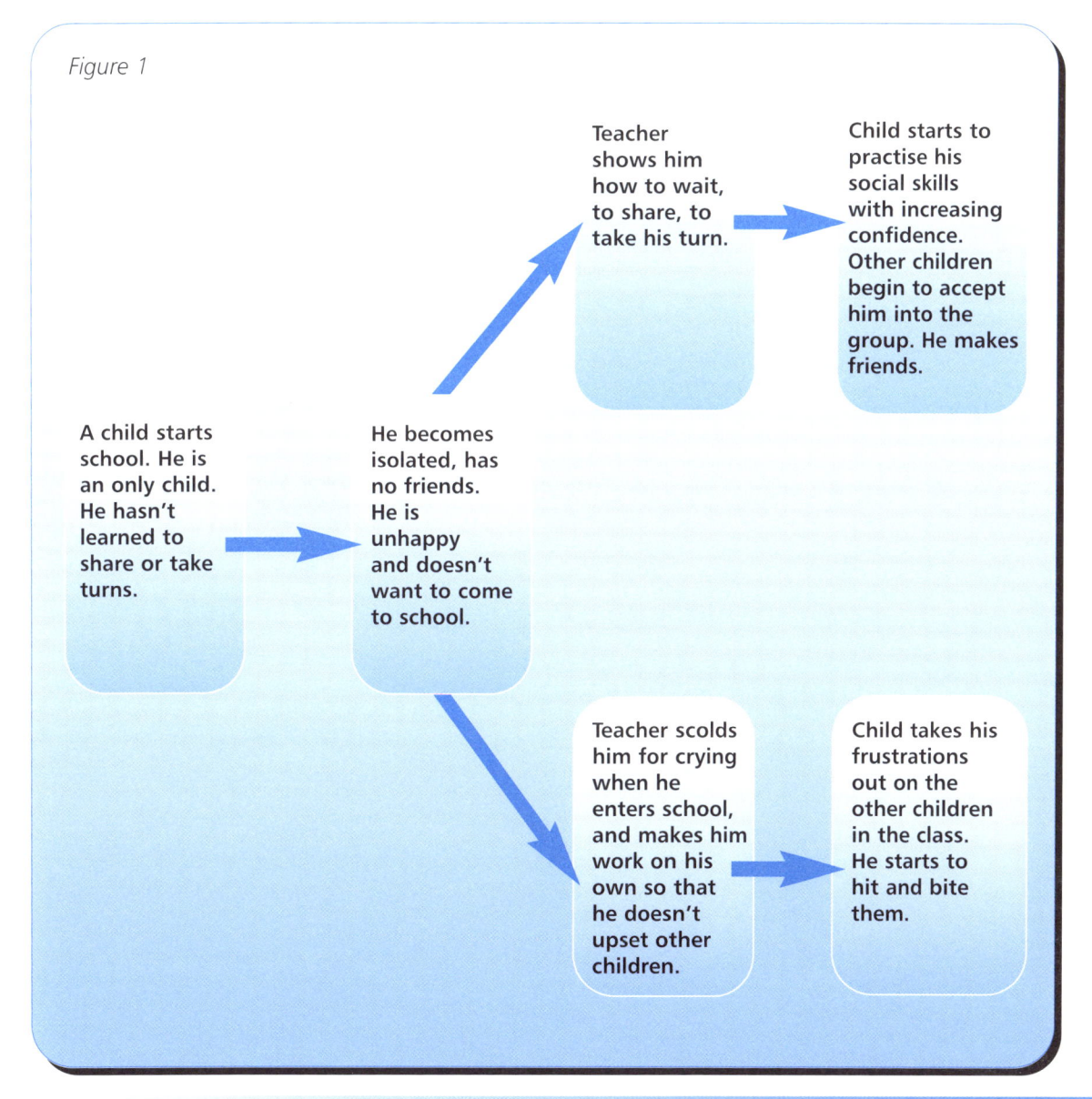

Figure 1

A child starts school. He is an only child. He hasn't learned to share or take turns. → He becomes isolated, has no friends. He is unhappy and doesn't want to come to school.

↗ Teacher shows him how to wait, to share, to take his turn. → Child starts to practise his social skills with increasing confidence. Other children begin to accept him into the group. He makes friends.

↘ Teacher scolds him for crying when he enters school, and makes him work on his own so that he doesn't upset other children. → Child takes his frustrations out on the other children in the class. He starts to hit and bite them.

The Positive Behaviour Handbook

SECTION ONE
Skills for teachers

The way we talk to children says much about our attitude towards their legal rights, as does the degree to which we involve them in decision-making and organisational issues. Many of the ideas discussed in the establishment phase of the year encompass children's right to be involved as active citizens in their learning community.

Children's basic rights in the classroom are

- the right to maximise their learning potential
- the right to be safe
- the right to be treated with respect.

But more than that, there is a moral right to which children are entitled – the right to play, work and learn in a friendly, helpful, safe school environment. Parents have the right to feel welcome and to know that their children are safe, well taught and cared for, and happy. Teachers have the right to teach in a school in which they are supported by colleagues, parents and the wider community.

It is helpful to all three of these groups if rights are explicitly acknowledged, displayed and reinforced. One of the most effective ways of doing this is for children to produce their own posters and cartoons illustrating the rights of each group, which can then be displayed around the school.

Tucked away at the end of the National Curriculum is the statement of values agreed by the National Forum for Values in Education. These values refer to the self, relationships, society and the environment. The non-statutory guidelines for PSHE and citizenship include a list of opportunities showing the breadth of experience children should have access to. The combination of the statement and the guidelines enshrines much of the moral, spiritual, social and cultural development that our children are entitled to in their learning experiences. Children's rights are central to our work in citizenship and PSHE, both in timetabled lessons and in their learning environment.

The promotion of positive behaviour has this development at its heart. Education is about far more than academic success. It is about enabling children to live purposefully and positively in society, to be part of a community, and to develop the skills, attitudes and some of the knowledge that will help them to decide for themselves what a worthwhile life will be. It is about enabling them to find mutuality in their relationships. And it is about them wanting to go on learning and helping others to learn too. With their self-esteem and confidence intact, they can experience a lifetime of learning.

Promoting positive behaviour provides the springboard for children to maximise their learning potential and to find purpose and enjoyment in the short time they spend with us at school.

Starting the year off well

Learning to be an effective teacher isn't easy. It's demanding – physically, mentally and emotionally – but it's also immensely rewarding. Sharing your working space and time with thirty young minds is a privilege. And it is this privilege that gives rise to what can feel like an overwhelming sense of responsibility.

It is important to acknowledge that in teaching there will always be limitless obligations. No teacher is able to meet all of them all of the time. From the outset we all have to prioritise.

In the continuous shifting of priorities and meeting of obligations, there is one constant – effective classroom management and the promotion of positive behaviour, in which there is a recognition that personal, social and health education is at the heart of all good teaching and learning. It has to be, because it is the springboard for everything that takes place in a primary school classroom. No matter how well you know your curriculum subjects or how much time you put into your assessment and recording systems, a lack of good classroom management and failure to promote positive behaviour will lead to a frustrated, unhappy class of learners – and an equally frustrated teacher.

Relationships are the key to making a class work as an effective teaching and learning community. From the outset, effective teachers focus on how to build rapport with the children in their classes. To feel secure in their learning, children need teachers who balance authority with warmth and who are consistent in their expectations.

So where do we start? Well, any consideration of how best to promote positive behaviour has to start with the basics of classroom organisation and management. This is because so much positive behaviour management relies first on the prevention of difficulties, thereby providing maximum opportunities for encouragement, praise and reward.

We summarise below the main areas for you to think about first. With these basics in place, you will have provided the groundwork for the promotion of positive behaviour and an effective teaching and learning community.

Classroom organisation and management

A well-organised classroom, which operates with consistent rules and routines, enables children to become independent learners and provides ample opportunities for the promotion of positive behaviour.

Being able to cope efficiently and effectively with the myriad demands of being a primary teacher has a major bearing on the quality of teaching and learning that takes place in the classroom. Consider the following key areas.

Use of furniture

Teachers sometimes need to remind themselves of the potential for using different combinations of classroom layout and the effect this can have on children's behaviour. As the year progresses you need to be prepared to consider whether the layout you started off with is appropriate for different types of activities and the needs of the children. Consider these main points.

- Children's positions in relation to the task and each other – taking into account learning objectives, social skills and any special needs.
- Lighting.
- Extraneous noise.

- Use of the sink.
- Access to tray units.
- Position of your desk and chair.
- Position of any spare tables and storage furniture. Spare tables covered with fabric can provide storage spaces beneath for materials, out of sight of the children and visitors.

Use of space

As you think about the organisation of the furniture in your room, it is particularly important that you plan to have a space where all the class can gather. If possible, this area should be carpeted.

Use of displays

Displays have different functions and are a fundamental tool in promoting positive behaviour. They can

- show the rules that have been agreed by the class and the other values that represent their class community – a large, active display of this kind is invaluable in the early days as a reference point for celebration when the children are doing wonderfully well at keeping to an agreed rule, and as a prompt for reminding children what has been agreed
- celebrate achievements
- demonstrate that all members of the class community, including the teacher, respect and value each other
- be informative
- be interactive
- act as a stimulus for learning, focus discussions and arouse curiosity, for instance at the beginning of a new topic
- encourage, enhance and praise the efforts of children for both academic and social achievements, eg. *'Our star of the week is Martin, for helping the children in Year 1 who got lost'*, *'Kylie has been a good friend this week'*, or *'We loved the poem Sam wrote this week'* displayed next to the relevant piece of work.

Materials and resources and children's access to them

These should be appropriate to the activity. They need to be sorted, labelled and stored and routines put in place so that they are readily accessible. You then use any opportunity to praise the use of the routines and the independent use of resources.

The materials need to provide for choice and differentiation for the range of ability in the class and specific special needs, ensuring equality of opportunity and access to the curriculum. They should be good quality wherever possible, for instance scissors that cut and pencils that are kept sharpened. Consumables need to be checked regularly so that they do not run out in the middle of a lesson, which can cause difficulties.

Time management and the need to prioritise

Lesson timings should be planned to prevent negative behaviour caused by children becoming bored by spending too long on the same activity. The needs and behaviour of the whole class must be given appropriate focus when an individual or group is demanding attention.

Creativity

Drama, dance, art and music all provide excellent ways into other learning, as well as requiring dedicated timetable space of their own. Plan for daily creative and physical activities – including the use of short activities that give young children's brains and bodies a break during sessions where they could be kept sitting still for too long. This helps children with a range of learning styles and concentration spans to remain interested and focused in class.

Consistent use of routines

Routines are essential for sound classroom organisation and management and promoting positive behaviour. Brainstorm with colleagues all the times during an average day when a routine helps – and share best practice. Ask the children for ideas on how to improve times that are notorious for causing disagreements and stress, such as wet playtimes.

High expectations and mutual respect

This is reflected in the care and respect given to

- the classroom environment
- class members and visitors
- messages included in displays.

High expectations are apparent in a classroom that is purposeful, task-orientated and relaxed, yet with an established sense of order. Children need to be supported and encouraged in their learning by their teacher's high, positive expectations. You provide a role model for the values, attitudes and good manners that everyone has agreed are important. The appearance and layout of the classroom should encourage positive attitudes from the children towards their learning, for example by celebrating their efforts and helping them to feel secure.

Class identity

Children should develop good reason to be proud of being in their class and feel they are part of a strong class community, which is readily identifiable by agreed values. The promotion of this class identity, associated with class members, can be a useful tool in the promotion of positive behaviour. Displays on the classroom door to welcome visitors can include a picture of each child and a brief outline of the values that everyone has agreed help to create a positive feeling, for instance 'Welcome to Class 4. We work hard and care for each other. We hope you enjoy your visit. Please ask any of us if you need help. We will try our best to help you!'

Every classroom should be a visually inviting and stimulating environment. How it is organised and exactly what is in it will depend on many factors, some of which are beyond your control. A bright and welcoming display that clearly sets out the values of the class, introduces class members and shares the rules, rights and responsibilities that have been agreed does much to help create a class identity. It can be added to and developed over time.

Grouping of children

Some behaviour difficulties arise as a direct result of inappropriate groupings of children for an activity. When considering the use of furniture and space, you should also try to develop an understanding of the appropriateness of different ways of working, and the developmental groupwork skills that need to be taught, nurtured and developed in primary school children. Whether to work as a whole class, individually with some one-to-one support, or cooperatively in groups (and if so the make-up of the group) is something that is learned and continually refined by teachers as they become more experienced.

Health and safety

Children will not respond positively to the teaching on offer if they are not comfortable and if their basic needs have not been met. You need to look at physical factors in the classroom.

- Airflow and temperature – is it stuffy and hot, or is there a chill wind whistling through ill-fitting window frames onto children near the window?
- What is the lighting like? Does it inhibit children's view of the board from some angles? Is the sun often in their eyes? Is it too dark for everyone to be able to see clearly?
- What routes have to be taken around the classroom to access resources? Classrooms should be free of clutter (as far as possible), clean and tidy. This can have a marked impact on the children when they first arrive at school. Children should be expected to leave work areas tidy when they have finished an activity.

A feel-good factor!

Developing a stock of sayings, phrases, responses, actions, short games and activities, and informal and formal rewards helps to establish a strong feel-good factor that motivates children. This can do much towards promoting positive behaviour.

Don't forget the aesthetics that will make a difference – the colours chosen for backing paper, plants in the room, inspirational posters and sayings and things that make you all smile!

Lesson planning

To successfully promote positive behaviour, consider the following as you prepare your lessons.

- **Learning objective.** What is it? Is it appropriate? Share this with children in childspeak appropriate to their age to ensure it has some meaning for them.
- **Activities.** Should they be the same? Differentiated? Whole-class? Groups? Individual? Why?
- **Content.** Planning, progression of and within activities, evaluation.
- **Children.** As independent learners, accessing own resources, being encouraged to think through problems in a logical way before asking for help.
- **Time management.** Between and during different tasks, the children's, your own, making time for plenaries.
- **Awareness of pressures and motivators.** Those created by the teacher, by peers, by content, by presentation, by the environment.
- **Assessment.** Opportunities to guide and ascertain next steps.
- **Teacher response and interaction with children.** Choice of words, body language, movement, intonation, volume, and the degree of acting required all need forethought.

Lesson management

Teachers are most effective in promoting positive behaviour when they have enough time

- for direct teaching
- to spend with each child
- to discuss work and children's responses
- to review, assess and celebrate achievements
- to reflect on their practice and the children's learning
- to enjoy their teaching and help children enjoy their learning.

Lesson management is concerned with the skills involved in managing and organising learning activities so that children's involvement in the lesson and their opportunities to learn are maximised. Effective lesson management maximises the opportunities for children to be purposefully engaged in the learning process and for the teacher to promote positive behaviour.

Key lesson management skills

Planning

Clear learning objectives, shared with children in language they understand and linked to past and future learning, help everyone to know what the point of the lesson is. Good planning ensures that the necessary materials and resources are prepared and to hand, minimising opportunities for negative behaviour from children who are bored or frustrated at not being able to do what they have been asked to do. A lesson that has been designed to sustain children's interest and involvement is one in which there will be ample opportunities for encouragement and reward. Content and teaching methods matched to the range of children's ability in the class will help to maximise the children's time spent on task.

Punctuality

You should always aim to be in the classroom, ready to promote and encourage positive behaviour, before the children arrive, rather than have to sort out problems that arise while they wait for you.

A positive start

A clear beginning – a signal or routine for gaining attention that children respond to – will help to focus children on the learning ahead. You should be centre-stage, using a clear voice, maintaining eye contact and scanning to ensure everyone is paying attention, pausing if necessary. If you begin without everyone paying attention you are signalling that this is acceptable and behaviour difficulties will arise from it.

The involvement of the children

Once the lesson has begun, interest must be sustained. Effective teachers convey in their tone and manner their own sense of curiosity and enthusiasm (and may be very good actors as far as this is concerned) and make links with previous work, for instance, 'Remember yesterday we looked at X. Thinking about what we said was most important, can anyone tell me what Y means?'

Pace and flow

Go too fast and some children will give up and switch off, missing important points or instructions and damaging their confidence as learners. Go too slow and children will become bored and distracted, and distract others. It's not easy, but getting the feel for the right pace is essential in good teaching. Unnecessary and minor interruptions need to be avoided.

Appropriate grouping

This needs careful planning to enable the learning objective to be achieved efficiently and effectively and to maximise your opportunities to promote positive behaviour.

- Whole-class teaching – this can take many forms, for instance exposition (teacher explains while children listen), demonstration, discussion, shared experiences, question and answer sessions, circletime, etc. Any whole-class teaching must involve children's participation.

- Groups – think of the different ways you may group children – random, friendship, ability, mixed ability, gender. Groupwork must have a clear focus and run alongside work on cooperative learning and social skills. Group tasks should have a time allocated to them and have explicit instructions and directions until established procedures are in place. You then need to consciously catch children being good within the group rather than waiting for communication and social difficulties to arise before you respond to the behaviour of the group.

  With ability grouping it is important that you remember that different curriculum areas will require different ability groups – a child will not be top or lowest ability in all subjects. Blanket groupings of children within a class by ability can give rise to behaviour difficulties if a child is either not sufficiently challenged or is over-paced.

- Pairs – the same considerations apply as to groups.

- Individual work.

Monitoring progress and providing feedback

You do this actively by circulating amongst children and asking very focused questions, relevant to the child's ability. Children must be encouraged to ask for help, but also to develop self-help strategies, for instance a 'What should I do if I'm stuck?' checklist. Children's questions highlight how best to sustain their involvement and progress in the lesson. Feedback during the lesson is helpful for identifying problems and indicating successful work and for providing ample opportunities for the positive reinforcement of children's behaviour.

Flexibility

Careful use of monitoring and feedback helps you to judge how the lesson is going. Sometimes teachers need to have the courage to make changes to their plans if it is clear that not all is going as expected and the class is not making progress in the lesson. Rigidly following such a lesson plan is likely to lead to behaviour management difficulties.

Managing time, movement and noise

Effective management of these three areas is essential if learning is to take place. Consistent use of routines is essential here. Agreed acceptable levels of noise need to be established and maintained. Referring frequently to displayed rules – both when they are being kept well and to deal

Lesson management is concerned with managing and organising learning activities so that children's involvement and their opportunities to learn are maximised

The Positive Behaviour Handbook

with behaviour problems – helps to promote the positive behaviour you are seeking. You will have to think critically about whether the noise is simply a requirement of the task or is unacceptably high, then decide how to model the desired behaviour and help children to learn how to monitor their noise level.

A positive and conclusive plenary

This helps children to feel good about their learning and understand what they have achieved. Giving children five minutes' notice that this is going to happen allows them to be ready to give feedback or share their work if they are asked to. This time can be used to reflect on and evaluate the activity, tell the children where the learning is going next and to draw the lesson to a close. Then all children can be involved in tidying away the activity and positive reinforcement of the relevant routines can take place.

Good relationships and rapport

This is one of the keys to a successful learning community. Children need to feel safe, valued and trusted. To be really successful in promoting positive behaviour, you need to

- be consistent
- be fair
- be firm
- be kind
- be reliable
- keep things in perspective and help children to do so too
- keep looking forward and help children to move on
- establish routines and patterns
- show yourself as a learner too.

A simple strategy to promote positive behaviour is to make full use of monitors, giving everyone a chance to do something to help the class community. Children love to help, usually take these duties seriously and carry them out well, particularly if such roles are clearly valued. Involving everyone in this helps to build responsibility and pride in the class. There is more advice on this in the chapter 'Taking responsibility'.

Have fun!

This is one of the most important aspects of all. Teachers can do this while still retaining their authority and the boundaries that help children to feel secure and flourish. It's true that play is a child's work, so learning to play with the children is time well invested in promoting positive behaviour. Finding reasons to smile and laugh every day – and helping children to see that learning is something we all do all the time – is one of the cornerstones of a successful, happy teaching and learning community.

Day one: rules and routines

The first day of the autumn term is when you are best able to establish both your authority and your warmth. At no other point in the school year are children so psychologically and developmentally ready for the establishment of how life in their classroom is going to be. Bill Rogers (1995) refers to the early days in the autumn term as '…the establishment phase of the year' (p71). He outlines the importance of the Four Rs – rules, rights, responsibilities and routines. Experience has shown that involving children in this establishment phase is crucial to how well they respond to the teacher's expectations for the class ethos. Children respond when they feel their views are valued and listened to.

To maximise their potential, children need to feel secure, happy and valued. This will help them to develop self-esteem, confidence and a positive self-image. This in turn will lead to positive behaviour and increased opportunities for effective teaching and learning to take place.

Children need to know – and actively experience – that sometimes you may not like aspects of their behaviour, but that you do like them as a person and can see all kinds of potential in them. This unconditional positive regard enables teachers to successfully build relationships with children that allow the promotion of positive behaviour. For some children the classroom may be the only place where they have a chance to feel secure and valued.

> At no other point in the school year are children so psychologically and developmentally ready for the establishment of how life in their classroom is going to be

So on day one you need to have planned carefully how you are going to establish your expectations, authority and warmth, in a session in which

- there is an explicit focus on the values that build a strong class community
- the Four Rs can be established – rules, rights, responsibilities and routines.

A plan for the consistent application of these is supported by the consistent use of rewards, sanctions and expectations, which is considered in detail in Section 3 of this book.

Consistency

Young learners need security. You can provide this through consistency in five key areas.

1. Rules.
2. Routines.
3. Rewards.
4. Sanctions.
5. Expectations.

1 Rules

For these to be properly understood and taken on board by the children, their purpose and appropriateness must be clear. They should be linked to work on communities and the understanding that all communities have rules to help them function. Talk to the children, in language appropriate to their age, about communities and ask them to identify communities to which they belong. You are aiming to make links to clubs that children attend and family life – any group of people who spend time together with a shared aim – and develop the children's understanding of how that group functions best. This discussion should be relatively short, lively and interesting for the children – you are not lecturing, but inviting them to explore the idea of groups of people sharing time and space together.

Aim for the understanding that an individual class – everyone within the four walls of your classroom – is a community. This in turn is part of the community of the school, which is part of the wider local community and so on.

Now choose a rule from the local community that everyone will immediately recognise, for example red traffic lights, and ask what the rule is. Once the rule has been explained, ask the children to think with you about why this rule exists. Aim to get to the idea of everyone having the right to travel reasonably safely on the road, which means that everyone driving a car has got the responsibility to keep other people on the road safe. The rule is there to help us – that's what rules are, things that are all around us in our lives to help us. Brainstorm other rules with which the children will identify, for example lining up at the supermarket checkout to pay for your shopping.

Continue to reinforce this idea so that children understand all the links, to retain a clear focus on the teaching points. You need to establish a notion of the triangle of rules, rights and responsibilities in language appropriate to the children's age and stage of development.

Make the link back to the classroom community.

- *What are our rights in the classroom?*

    Example – to learn in a place in which we feel safe and respected.

- *So what are our responsibilities to each other?*

    Example – to help each other to be safe and feel respected. At this point you will have to ask what this means in order to make the words practical and relevant to the children. 'We help each other to be safe' is the positive wording of rules that could be negatively expressed as 'No punching, no kicking, no spitting, no being unkind to one another'.

- *We therefore need some rules.*

    Example – use one from the classroom. Take other examples from the outside world to show that the notion of rules, rights or responsibilities is not something unique to school life – it affects us all on every day of our lives.

This can then be used to establish the rules needed in our community – the classroom. You need to know the rules you are aiming for, but ensure that they are elicited from the children. The children will usually provide them in negative terms, such as 'No talking when the teacher is talking', and 'No kicking'. Rephrasing them in the positive is important, so that this is the message you regularly share and promote with the children, eg. 'We listen carefully', 'We help each other to be safe'. It can be helpful to show both initially, eg. 'No calling out or interrupting'/'We listen carefully', to help reinforce children's understanding.

The rules should be presented on a large display that also makes reference to the idea of a community which has rights and responsibilities. This display should be put up by the end of day one, so that the rules are there to refer to from the next day onwards. They must be referred to regularly, particularly when the class is doing well at keeping a rule – look out for this so that you can promote the positive behaviour by celebrating it.

An announcement such as 'You are all doing so brilliantly at keeping this rule that I think we ought to pack up this lesson two minutes early and have a game' will be met with universal delight and will only take two minutes from your lesson time, but you will have invested so much more in your promotion of positive behaviour. When a rule is being broken the display can be referred to with the whole class as a reminder of what was agreed, and why, and privately with an individual child who needs more focus.

The school rules may also be displayed in your classroom. These will be very similar to the class rules, but extra class rules will have come out of the discussion, so don't be tempted to just put the school rules up. They will have been seen by some children for years and will not have the impact that you want. Make your rule display HUGE and positive! For this first day it will save time to have already prepared all the signs about the community and the values you are promoting – they will all come out of the discussion.

There will be a need for explicit reminders of rules that apply at specific times. For example, a display on 'What can we do at wet playtimes?' can include all the activities the children can engage in, but alongside a 'Helping each other to be safe' rule or statement it will be helpful to have a specific reminder such as 'Remember – NO scissors to be used during wet playtimes'.

Talking about the rules can lead into a brief discussion of the sanctions that would be fair to apply if somebody kept breaking the rules that everyone has agreed are important. Section 3 of this book looks in detail at sanctions. A brief positive comment and an outline of all the good things you are looking forward to enjoying with the class over the year can help to balance this discussion of sanctions and set it in context.

So, in essence, rules need to

- have a clear purpose and so be seen to be fair – a crucial factor to children – and be set in the context of everyday life
- be clarified, displayed and consistently enforced and celebrated
- be not too lengthy a list
- be positively phrased and expressed simply – the 'negative' childspeak alongside may help to remind children what this means
- be supportive of the school rules
- be enforceable
- be enforced with consistency and fairness
- relate clearly to routines.

> You need to know the rules you are aiming for, but ensure that they are elicited from the children

The Positive Behaviour Handbook

2 Routines

It is through routines that we teach the rules and consolidate the responsibilities required for children to develop self-discipline and become independent learners.

Routines help a class to run smoothly and are essential to good classroom management. Routines need to be explained, modelled and constantly rehearsed, reinforced and encouraged. As with rules, clear reasons for routines must be given so that they become second nature to the children. This provides ample scope for the promotion of positive behaviour.

There are endless opportunities during a primary school day when routines can be used to make everyone's lives easier and to maximise time. There are some key points at which children need to know clearly what the routines are for their behaviour. These are

- when they enter and leave any space
- the signal used by the teacher to gain attention
- at break and lunchtimes
- for everyday activities such as sharpening pencils/going to the toilet/hanging up coats/retrieving lunch boxes
- for gaining the teacher's attention
- for gaining access to resources
- appropriate noise levels at different working times.

Reminders should be given early on in the establishment of these routines and every now and then to consolidate them, for example 'Before we go into the music room, who can remind us of what we need to do once we're inside?' It is essential to encourage children who remember the routines without being reminded, as you do those who keep the rules or show good manners without being reminded, for example 'Thank you for remembering to put that away'.

Use these key points to create successful routines.

- Be on time and prepared at the beginning of teaching sessions.
- Begin each day in the same way – both what the children are expected to do and what you do.
- Have a positive start, which looks at the day ahead in an encouraging way.
- End each day in the same way – both what the children are expected to do and what you do.
- Have a positive ending, which reflects on the successes of the day. This can include the difficult things that were worked through. 'Clearing up' and 'being ready to go' routines need to be explicitly taught. A routine for saying hello to each other in the mornings and goodbye at the end of the working day does much to help develop positive relationships.

3, 4 and 5 Rewards, sanctions and expectations

Details on these areas can be found in Section 3 of this book.

Good manners

As old-fashioned as it may sound, this is an important area in which children can develop the social skills and self-discipline that they need to live and work with others. Low expectations from the teacher and lack of awareness by the children of the role that manners play can make a significant difference to classroom life and the children's attitude towards it.

It is crucial that you don't simply expect, assume or demand good manners from children. It is not for teachers to imply that a lack of good manners is wrong and you must, of course, be sensitive to cultural and social differences. What is important is that we simply understand that children may not be experiencing basic good manners as part of their everyday life. This, in turn, means that teachers need to teach and encourage good manners as part of the framework of rules, rights and responsibilities described above.

The basics – 'please', 'thank you', 'excuse me', waiting your turn, etc. – may not be at all basic or obvious to many children. So this is a key area in which you need to promote positive behaviour. For example, notice and thank the child who asks to come into the classroom when you are in there at lunchtime. Quietly remind the child who runs through your conversation with a colleague or another child and ask them to move around you. Be a good role model when good manners are shown to you by thanking the child with a smile.

Never take good behaviour for granted. Promoting positive behaviour requires you to be on the lookout for, and to celebrate, the good behaviour around you.

References

Rogers, B (1995) *Behaviour Management – A whole school approach*. Gosford, Australia: Scholastic.

> It is not for teachers to imply that a lack of good manners is wrong

Circletime

What is circletime?

Circletime is an activity specifically designed to enhance the self-esteem of everyone who takes part in it, while addressing a range of interpersonal, intrapersonal and organisational issues. It involves everyone, including any adults in the room, sitting in a circle so that all can make eye contact. The circle format has symbolised equality and mutual respect throughout the centuries.

There is certainly a link between children's self-esteem, their behaviour and the extent to which they achieve their academic potential. Circletime can contribute hugely to the promotion of positive behaviour by having a direct influence on children's self-esteem. The benefits are wide ranging, both for children and teachers.

For children, the benefits include

- opportunities for increased confidence and self-esteem, allowing children to rise to the challenge of learning experiences
- a time to explore feelings and listen to each other
- the experience of being listened to and having their opinion valued
- activities that help the class to gel
- activities that address common serious issues such as bullying
- enhanced experience of being part of a class community
- a structured time to get to know the teacher and other children better
- enhanced speaking and listening skills, which can be used across the curriculum
- the development of a class of children who are mutually supportive and who are building positive relationships
- a happier, friendlier school
- having fun while learning.

For the teacher, the benefits include

- opportunities to develop knowledge and understanding of individual children and of how the class gels as a whole
- greater trust in the capabilities of the children in the class
- enhanced understanding of the children's perspective on their learning
- opportunities for professional reflection and development, by seeing herself through the eyes of the children
- a way of structuring class discussion time and problem-solving activities
- a way of teaching across the curriculum, for example role-play in literacy, debate in history, discussion in PSHE
- the development of a class of children who are mutually supportive and who are building positive relationships
- a happier, friendlier school
- having fun while teaching.

Key characteristics are that

- everyone's contribution is of equal value
- everyone has the right to participate, the responsibility to listen and the opportunity to speak.

Activities may include

- cooperative games and activities
- problem-solving
- celebrations
- discussions
- role-play
- sharing of feelings.

Sessions are best structured as a short warm-up activity, followed by the main focus and finally a short closing activity. Circletime can be developed as a strategy across the whole school, focusing on specific skills such as active listening in the early years and working towards a focus on debating in Year 6. Within this, focus time will still be allocated to the development of a range of personal, social and health education skills throughout all year groups, allowing children to continue to develop positive relationships and heightened self-esteem.

> Circletime can be developed as a strategy across the whole school, focusing on specific skills such as active listening

How does it work?

To be effective, circletime must operate within an agreed framework of rules. It also needs to have a clear focus, otherwise it can degenerate into simply a sharing of news or a meaningless couple of rounds or games.

The rules, and what happens when class members choose not to follow the rules, need to be agreed with the children. Typically, the rules will be those that encourage and demonstrate mutual respect. The formulation of these rules may be part of the content of the first circletime session. They will include the following.

- All participants taking equal responsibility for solving problems.
- Everyone taking turns to speak, listen and voice their concerns. With younger children this is helped by passing an object to indicate that it is that person's turn to speak (for example, in a round).
- Everyone having the right to decline to speak. If there is a round they should say 'pass' so that everyone realises that they are choosing not to contribute. At the end the person who started the round can ask if anyone who passed has anything they'd like to say, giving them a little more thinking time.
- Time being provided for everyone to offer help and encouragement to others and to ask the group for help about their own concerns.
- Sitting at equal height in a circle in which everyone can make eye contact.

There are some absolute musts.

- Respecting other people's right to speak and not putting anyone down.
- Asking for help with a problem but not verbally attacking and blaming anyone in the circle for the problem. For example, a child may say 'I'm being pushed around by someone in the class and would like some help' rather than naming the child.
- Including a positive focus and, ideally, an element of fun in every session. Circletime can become an intimidating experience if it is only ever used to address problems which do not have their emphasis on positive resolutions.

The teacher's role

The teacher's role is that of a facilitator to the group, encouraging children to feel that they have the ability to solve the problem that is confronting the group or to offer an idea. Of course, in the early days teachers will spend much time promoting the positive behaviour required for circletime to be successful and ensuring that the fundamental rules are followed. Their most crucial role at this stage is to introduce and support a range of strategies which allow the development of cooperative group skills, honesty and trust from the children.

Practicalities

One of the things that can put teachers off circletime is the need to move furniture to make the space. Their concerns about doing this relate to the time it will take and the safety and behaviour of the children. In some classrooms, particularly those for younger children, there is a large enough carpet space for a circle to be formed without moving furniture (although you may still wish to use chairs for the children and yourself to sit on). But with older children, who need to be sitting on chairs and whose furniture takes up more space in the class, there will be a certain amount of furniture to be moved.

On the first few occasions circletime will inevitably take longer to organise. However, approaching it as part of the children's learning of social and collaborative skills will enable you to plan it much as you would any other activity. It is useful if early circletime sessions can have an emphasis on enjoyment – some active listening skills games and partner work. This will encourage the children to be enthusiastic about the idea of working in a circle and enable you to promote the positive behaviour required for moving into a circle quickly and safely.

It is far preferable to use the classroom whenever possible, rather than a larger space such as the hall. It has the advantages of being a safe environment where the children are likely to feel more confident, being a more intimate space and being available for circletime whenever you feel it is appropriate. Remember that while your circletime sessions will have a ritual that indicates the beginning and end, working in this format is likely to be very useful for

Guidelines for helping circletimes to be successful

- [ ] Always have a planned structure, but as you become more experienced and confident at running circletimes be prepared to be flexible so that you can respond appropriately to any major concerns or issues that are presented.

- [ ] Help children to understand the notion of confidentiality, but within the realistic constraints that are placed upon you in the situation. So, for example, children should be encouraged to say things that concern them, but if it is something very personal or upsetting they may want to speak to you privately about it first or afterwards. Circletime sometimes suffers from being labelled 'quasi-counselling' by those who misunderstand this aspect of promoting confidentiality within the circle. You are aiming to encourage children to feel safe enough to talk without the fear of someone laughing about what they said in the playground afterwards.

- [ ] Keep the sessions short enough to sustain interest and desire for the next session. 10–15 minutes will be sufficient for younger children, 25–30 minutes for older children. This can be extended if work in other curriculum areas is being included, for example a discussion, partner work and feedback in RE.

- [ ] Circletime must not exist in a vacuum. It is therefore important when problem-solving and sharing concerns that you follow up on issues that arise. It is a way for the class to address problems together, find solutions, and then put them into action.

- [ ] Make them fun! Vary them by including different types of activities *(see What can you do in a circletime?).*

- [ ] Take the time to reflect on and evaluate them together, so that you can all suggest how they can be improved.

- [ ] With very withdrawn children, consider letting them know in advance about a non-threatening round (eg. my favourite TV programme or favourite food) so that they have enough time to think of a contribution. Another idea is the use of puppets, controlled by the teacher, to whom withdrawn and shy children may speak, so that the puppet can do the talking for them.

- [ ] Start and end circletimes with an enjoyable game or round, or a calming activity, as appropriate.

---

other learning such as music, RE, some history and literacy lessons and PSHE.

If the children are very young or moving the furniture is particularly difficult, consider the use of older 'circletime helpers' who may be able to help you arrange, set out or put away the furniture if this can be conveniently timetabled (such as before or after a break). Where possible, however, use the forming of the circle as an important part of the children helping and learning together. You may find that working in a circle is a particularly successful way of conducting several lessons. If so, you may wish to use a classroom layout such as a horseshoe for other lessons to make it easy to form a circle, and only move the furniture into grouped tables or other layouts for specific grouped activities.

What can you do in a circletime?

Circletime doesn't have to be limited to talking about issues and difficulties. It is the ideal opportunity to promote positive behaviour through the use of a range of activities and games that develop children's collaborative, personal and social skills, along with their self-esteem and confidence and their ability to communicate effectively with each other. Here are some ideas for activities.

Games

These are useful for helping a class to gel, developing trust and cooperation, providing enjoyment and breaking tension, and encouraging the development of self-discipline and keeping to agreed rules.

Rounds – passing a special object

These sessions, where an object is passed from speaker to speaker in turn, allow a focus on a special thought, subject or issue. Sometimes the beginning of the sentence is provided, for example 'One thing that makes me smile is…', 'Something that I would like to change in our class is…'. At other times just the subject is offered. Nobody is allowed to comment on what anyone says. At the end the teacher can ask anyone who 'passed' whether they'd like to make a comment.

It can be particularly helpful to have a circletime when a new member joins the class and a round

> Have a circletime when a new member joins the class and a round in which everyone says their name and introduces the person next to them

in which everyone says their name and introduces the person next to them. Seat them next to the teacher, so that they say their own name and introduce their teacher. Straightaway they will have contributed as much as everyone else to the activity. This can then be developed into other activities that will help the child to be welcomed to the class, without too much explicit focus on them, which would be stressful for some children. For example, after the introductory activity there could be a game in which children participate individually, but which aims to help children to gel. There could then be partner work.

Brainstorming

This can be a useful opportunity to take everyone's contribution without the ideas being categorised as useful or not, and for considering ideas such as 'How can you tell if someone is listening to you?'

Working in pairs

Working in pairs, children can talk and listen to each other (with a designated time given to each) on a given subject. Each child then has to summarise the other's information and feed it back to the group. This is a useful technique for working on active listening skills.

Celebrating work

Children can nominate each other for praise for anything at all which deserves the recognition of the group. So, for example, it might be how kind one child was to another who was feeling down, or a child's opinion that another child's piece of art was really good.

Drama

Role-play allows children to express feelings, practise empathising with others, try out different ways of behaving in a situation and explore problems. Mime helps children understand that we communicate with our whole bodies, not just with words. Drama helps children to play creatively.

Discussion/debate

The consideration of different points of view needs skills of give and take which many adults have not mastered! Circletime is the ideal environment in which to practise this skill.

What do you think about...?

A question or moral dilemma can be put forward, which everyone has to think about and respond to if they feel comfortable doing so. It is important in this exercise that the teacher does not have 'the right answer'. Children are used to looking to teachers for answers but that would defeat the purpose of this activity.

Evaluation and reflection

Children need to learn that thinking about something, taking stock and deciding what can be learned from a situation are skills that take time and practice to develop. Working in this way in a group helps children to realise that there is always more than one interpretation of a situation.

Calming/feel-good

Circletime can be used deliberately to lift children's spirits at stressful times. Alternatively, it can be used to create small windows of time in which children learn how to be still, calm and relaxed. Breathing and visualisation activities can do much to help children who are working towards positive behaviour and everyone will enjoy and benefit from them.

Circletime activities

Some of the many collections of circletime activities are available from the following suppliers.

Jenny Mosley Consultancies
8 Westbourne Road
Trowbridge
Wiltshire BA14 0AJ
www.circle-time.co.uk

Lucky Duck Publishing
34 Wellington Park,
Clifton
Bristol BS8 2UW
www.luckyduck.co.uk

Southgate Publishers Ltd
Glebe House
Church Street
Crediton
Devon EX17 2AF
www.southgatepublishers.co.uk

Talking to children

What we say and how we say it

The outcome of much of what we do when we manage children's behaviour and promote positive behaviour is affected by our choice of language. What we say – and how we say it – makes a real difference to the child, in particular to his passive state.

Consider how these two ways of saying the same thing may make a child feel, depending on the tone and body language used.

'OK, now don't forget to sit on the carpet. I don't want to see people wandering around or being generally silly. Do you understand?'

or

'Well done for lining up so sensibly. Remember to sit on the carpet area when we go in.'

It's important to analyse language use – both our own and that of other professionals with whom we are working. In doing so, we must also consider

- tone
- volume
- timing – in particular, pausing
- eye contact
- body language – in particular, the posture we assume and the gestures we use
- proximity to the children
- the context of the situation – for example, whether it's on the playground or in a whole-class lesson.

In other words it's not just what we say, but how we say it to children that is important. All the points listed above make a difference to the message the child receives when they hear the words spoken.

When you consider that there are dozens of different uses for our language during an average day, children need to understand what we are asking of them and we need to know what we are trying to achieve with the words and delivery we are using.

Are we

- reminding
- requesting
- directing
- gaining attention
- holding attention
- questioning
- explaining
- repeating
- redirecting
- diverting attention
- clarifying
- establishing understanding
- sympathising
- empathising
- encouraging
- joking.

SKILLS FOR TEACHERS

It's not just what we say, but how we say it to children that is important

The Positive Behaviour Handbook 21

> A smile goes a long way in demonstrating that you are expecting the desired behaviour

Anybody who teaches knows that managing children's behaviour – and continually working hard at promoting positive behaviour – can be an emotional issue. It can touch on our fundamental beliefs and values – in fact our very philosophy of what it is to be a teacher. So the language we use is potentially a difficult area, because if teachers are feeling stressed, tired, disappointed or angry they can give a message that can undo much of their previous good work.

It's important to give prior consideration and planning to our use of language – and to practise taking a few moments to stop and think before responding to an incident involving behaviour management. Equally, children will know our hearts aren't in it if we praise without conveying the appropriate emotion when promoting positive behaviour.

When using language to promote positive behaviour, we will be encouraging, explaining, reminding, and requesting. This will move into questioning and directing. As with the use of sanctions, it is important that we use an approach that Rogers (1995, p34) refers to as moving from '…least to most intrusive'. Managing children's behaviour will always involve much reminding.

Reminding

It sounds obvious, but reminding is an important part of effective classroom management. Children, like many adults, are forgetful. Early on in the year and often after every holiday, weekend, or supply teacher, children will need numerous reminders about the agreed rules and routines that apply in the classroom.

A simple prompt such as 'We agreed a rule for lining up, so please use it' said positively, with the expectation that the children are going to do what they should, and giving them a chance to do it before you give your attention to the matter again, can be a positive reminder, preventing an escalation of problems.

This needs to be combined with positive reinforcement of the behaviour when it occurs without a reminder – 'Well done for remembering to use our rule for lining up', or a little flattery to encourage – 'It's so wonderful to know I have a class of such responsible children. Thanks for using our rule for lining up'.

When we have reminded a child or class about a rule, it helps to promote positive behaviour if we are on the lookout for that rule being kept without the reminder, so that we can acknowledge it. This may be as discreet and private as a smile, or a 'thumbs up'.

Occasionally, reminders may need to sound less positive, for example if safety is an issue. 'Stop!' said with a firmer tone should still be followed with a reminder. 'We agreed a rule for working with scissors, so use it, please.'

Often the reminder can be brief – 'Sensibly, please'.

Initially, remind children before the behaviour is required, for instance with a routine. A smile goes a long way in demonstrating that you are expecting the desired behaviour, rather than looking for a confrontation.

Remember to praise children when they follow routines without being reminded. Using 'Remember to…' is a more positive way of reminding than 'Don't forget to…'. As we all use the phrases a lot, the former is a good habit to get into. It is useful to think about all the instructions that we usually start with a 'Don't' or a 'No' and reword them. They can be practised until the positive statement becomes the more natural response.

22 The Positive Behaviour Handbook

Directing and instructing positively

- 'Don't think of a green elephant.' What are you now thinking of? It's the same with children – we get better results if the language we use promotes and directs the child to the desired behaviour, rather than the undesired. So, 'Don't leave your books in a mess on the table' becomes 'Place your books neatly in the tray'.

- We need to turn negatives into positive reminders, just like we do with the rules when we're establishing them. 'Stop being so careless with the paint pots' becomes 'Carefully with the paint pots, thank you'.

- Instructions need to be clear and concise. 'For goodness sake, how many times have I had to tell you to concentrate? Look this way instead of daydreaming out of the window!' becomes 'Martin, Anna, look this way, please'.

- Instructions need to show any steps required.
'No, you can't do your painting because you haven't finished your story' becomes 'Yes, when you've finished your story, then you can do your painting' or 'Yes you can, as soon as you've finished this piece of work'.

Consider some other useful approaches

- Pausing – for example when gaining the children's attention. The pause in this instance can act as a brief waiting time, supported by confident body language that says 'OK everyone, I'm expecting you to listen now that I've got your attention'. Rushing our language can prevent us from holding children's attention, or lead to us speaking over low-level chatter, which is not promoting the positive behaviour required.

- Using silence. Consciously leaving spaces in dialogue allows for the kind of reflection that encourages active listening, a considered response and can decrease emotional tension.

- Favourite class phrases – using a range of these can be very successful, particularly if the class have helped invent them! Unusually long words, often made up, to describe something fantastic or unusually interesting can make a class smile.

- Gentle, kind humour. Aim to build a class that laughs and smiles every day, but never at anyone's expense.

Compliments

Taking opportunities to compliment children, for instance 'There's some excellent work going on in the back corner of the room…', 'I can tell how hard you're considering what John's suggested – well done' is encouraging. With those less inspired to get on with the task in hand, reminders such as 'I'm looking forward to reading your opinion in five minutes' time, Emma', which imply that very shortly you will be specifically focusing on the child, can be useful.

Repeat, rephrase

It's easy to forget how confusing everyday phrases can be when used in different contexts. The repetition and slight rephrasing of questions allows children to have another chance to understand. Visual reminders such as signs and written instructions will help children with a predominantly visual learning style. Kinaesthetic learners may need to consolidate an instruction with movements that remind them of the steps involved.

We need to be clear about what we expect. For example, if we ask for silence is that really what we mean, or do we simply want it to be quiet. Children need to learn the difference – so we need to express it clearly.

The Positive Behaviour Handbook

Respect

As with everything we do, we must fundamentally respect children by the way in which we communicate with them and ensure that other adults in the room understand that this is the approach we use.

The way adults talk to each other, about children and in front of them, is crucial. The self-esteem of the child is paramount. Children hear more than adults think they hear, understand more than adults think they understand and learn when adults are unaware that they are learning. Teacher talk leaves its mark long after the words have been said.

Promoting positive behaviour through our language ensures that the messages we leave behind nurture children's inner strength and growing sense of self-discipline.

SECTION TWO
Involving the children

We want our children to become adults who show respect for other people, their beliefs and their opinions. But first children have to learn to respect themselves.

They need to be given respect by those around them. They need to know that their opinions are valued and that their contributions will be accepted gracefully. They need to appreciate that criticism can be a healthy way to learn from their experiences and that there is a positive way in which criticism can be given so that it doesn't cause offence or belittle the other person. Children need to know what they can do, how much they have learned and their contribution to the life of the school must be acknowledged and valued. In this kind of atmosphere children can feel self-confident and self-esteem can be raised.

Bee (1989) lists the characteristics of children with high self-esteem compared to those with low self-esteem. The following three are relevant to primary schools.

- Higher achievement in school.
- Taking responsibility for their own success or failure.
- Having more friends.

She looks at the role of the parents in the creation of this child with high self-esteem, summarising the research on this issue. We can take her key points and apply them equally well to the adult in the classroom. She says that children who develop high self-esteem are surrounded by '…firm but reasoned control, positive encouragement of independence and a warm and loving atmosphere' (p366).

In this section we will concentrate on two ways in which you can give the children in your class this 'positive encouragement of independence'.

- Through enabling the children to play an active part in their own learning.

  The 'Developing high self-esteem' chapter explores ways to enable the children to appreciate their own learning and achievements, to know what it is they have accomplished and to develop evaluation skills so that they can interact with you in the assessment of their work.

- Through giving responsibility to the children.

  The chapter 'Taking responsibility' gives practical advice on handing responsibility to children for managing their classroom environment, and ideas for increasing their level of responsibility so that they can support other children in the school or in their own class. It also contains suggestions for ways in which children can be enabled to make informed choices about their actions, and their reactions to people and events that they might come across.

Developing high self-esteem and learning about criticism

When children are hurt or offended they may react inappropriately. Some children react to accidental bumps and knocks by lashing out at the perpetrator. Others may overreact to any form of criticism, even to a piece of work being marked as wrong. These children haven't learned how to deal with criticism about themselves.

There are also occasions when children jeer at someone else's mistake or even pass comments about another person's physical appearance. These children haven't learned to control their critical nature. All of these groups of children have yet to learn how to give and receive criticism in an empathic way, and to know that criticism can be a constructive part of life and learning.

In all aspects of life children need to be able to think in critical ways. Young children in particular, associate criticism of their idea or their opinion with criticism of themselves, and can be very hurt by this. It is our task to help children to learn the healthy use of criticism. At the same time, we have to enable them to raise their level of self-esteem so that they are not offended by innocent or well-intentioned words and actions.

One way is to look at how we can use self-evaluation with children. We can involve the children in the process of assessment and evaluation of their work and their behaviour by helping them to develop the skills they need. We set targets for children in literacy and in numeracy, perhaps for their behaviour or for their IEPs. We assess children every time we mark their work, we hand out rewards as we observe progress or effort, we write reports about them and speak to their parents. Instead of doing all this to the children, it would help to develop their self-knowledge and self-respect if we were to find ways to involve them in this process. This means developing the skills the children will need to participate in this in a meaningful way.

This chapter looks at why the children need to develop the following skills and gives some practical classroom applications for you to use.

Children need to

- be able to see things from other people's points of view
- be able to give reasons for their opinion
- learn to use constructive language
- experience lots of different kinds of questions to make them think and to show them how to question and think for themselves
- know what it is they are evaluating
- be able to recognise their own achievement
- learn how to evaluate their work.

There are activities and approaches that you can use in the classroom to let them practise giving and receiving criticism in non-threatening ways and so assist the development of high self-esteem.

Children need to be able to see things from other people's points of view

This is crucial if children are to develop acceptable social behaviour. Even babies show some evidence of empathy – they can look concerned or upset if a parent's facial expression shows distress or pain. This is already well established in many of the children in our classrooms. Other children don't have this ability to the same degree, and need our support if they are to develop it. In chapter eight of Early Childhood Education (1987), Tina Bruce explores the development of what she terms 'decentration' as a way of enabling children to have moral values and moral standards. Part of the role of the adult is to help children take these latent abilities and act upon them. If this hasn't happened at home, you as the teacher need to find ways to move children along this path.

The ideas you can develop in your own classroom will depend upon the age and ability of the children. Think about whether your children would prefer to share their ideas verbally or whether they have good literacy skills and would be happier to commit their ideas to paper first. You can work in small groups and then share one or two ideas with the whole class. You may need to

- put yourself in the hot seat a few times to demonstrate to the children
- support them by providing some questions
- intervene if children diverge too far from the original intentions of the activity.

As with all things, provide variety and praise all efforts.

Children need to be able to give reasons for their opinion

Children who can give a reasoned and reasonable explanation for their actions or behaviour can defend themselves in non-combative ways. They can say what they are feeling and why. They can ask another child to stop doing something or take their concern to an adult and give a clear message.

In discussions and debates in the classroom children can learn how to put together their argument. It's not sufficient to say 'because I like it' or 'because I do'. Children need to learn how to back up their opinion with reasoned arguments and in a confident manner.

A simple technique put forward by Edward de Bono (Teach Your Child How to Think, 1992) is PMI.

P   **PLUS**
M   **MINUS**
I   **INTERESTING**

He explains this as being '…a perception-broadening tool (attention-directing) which forces a thinker to explore the situation before coming to a judgement' (p128). Start by using this as a whole-class, oral exercise during a lesson or as a shared evaluation tool after a session. When children are confident, they can use it individually to evaluate their response to a unit of work in, for example, history or science. It should always be used in this specific order, firstly looking for the Plus points of an argument or discussion, then the Minus points and finally the Interesting points.

Example activities to help children see things from other people's points of view

Children work in small groups. Over a series of short sessions each can have a turn at being in the hot seat. The others in the group have to ask questions and the person in the hot seat must answer as if he is that person.

Imagine you are one of the ugly sisters in the story of Cinderella.

- Why are you so mean to Cinderella?
- Do you think you are better than her?
- Do you like being called ugly?
- How did you feel when the shoe fitted Cinderella and not you?

What does it feel like to be

- a lost kitten?
- a discarded teddy bear?
- an old lady living on her own in a block of flats?
- the winner of a lot of money?
- a mummy with a new baby?

Children write down a list of words or phrases.

They could work in pairs until they gain confidence in doing this.

The Positive Behaviour Handbook

Example activities to help children to give reasons for their opinion

> **Should people be allowed to chop down the rainforest to make farmland available?**
>
> **Should parents be allowed to drive into the school grounds when bringing children to school?**
>
> *Discuss these questions using the PMI technique.*
>
> P   PLUS – the good things.
>
> M   MINUS – the bad things.
>
> I   INTERESTING – things which are neither good nor bad. Include observations and comments.

> **Look at a painting together. Do you like it? Why?**
>
> *Pose some challenging questions which could be adapted for other situations.*
>
> **Would it be better if the lady's hat was a different colour?**
>
> **Why did the artist use oil paint rather than watercolours?**
>
> **If you were painting this, would you have put that small dog just there?**
>
> **Do you think it would be better if the artist had made it lighter?**

> *When reading to the whole class, or when reading with an individual child, spend time sharing opinions about the book.*
>
> **What was your favourite part?**
>
> **Were you surprised when…?**
>
> **What did you think was going to happen when she fell into the icy pond?**
>
> **Would you have made Tom so bad-tempered if you were writing it? Do you think it helped the story along for him to be like that?**

Children need to learn to use constructive language

Our aim is that the children should be able to comment or give an opinion in acceptable, non-condemnatory ways. This means that we need to set them the example we want them to follow. Children are learning whether we are teaching them or not. They are picking up the subliminal messages in our body language and in our tone of voice as well as in the words and phrases we choose to use with them.

The chapter 'Talking to children' went into this in greater depth, but we now need to think about how the ways in which we comment on children's work and effort are influencing the children's own use of criticism – whether it is of themselves or of those around them.

● When you add a written comment to the children's work, make it a positive but helpful statement.

   'You have structured this story in a clever way. The way you added the character of Jonas into the middle section was very effective. I think that the last paragraph would have been better if you had stopped after the words 'never again', to let the reader draw his own conclusions.'

   'This flow chart shows very clearly what happens to chocolate when you heat it. Remember to add a title to your work.'

   You can try posing a question at the end of the comment so that children can respond.

   'The character of Green-eye works well in this story, but I'm not sure about your choice of the name. Do you think it could improve your story if the name was less obvious?'

● When you are having a class discussion seeking opinions or ideas, find ways to encourage all the children to participate. Children need opportunities to practise committing their opinions to the public ear and expressing themselves so that they don't offend others. There are ways in which you can provide these opportunities so that the hesitant children in your class have an equal chance alongside the more vocal youngsters.

   'Tell your neighbour the answer to this next question.'

   'Tell the person next to you why you think it's wrong to keep a ten-pound note that you find on the Post Office floor.'

   Then you can brainstorm the idea with the whole class, writing up the children's responses for all to see. The shy child who whispered his idea to his vocal neighbour will then feel pride when he sees his answer up on the board.

- Give the children time to talk in a small group and note down three shared ideas or opinions on sticky notes. Stick these around the room. The shy child can be anonymous, the insecure child will have the comfort of the small group to help him phrase his idea appropriately, the loud child will be reduced to a limited offering. The child who doesn't actually know the answer will be able to share in the success of his group – nobody will know he didn't contribute personally, but he will have picked up some ideas from his group and he can now share them as if they were his own.

- When listening to children's ideas and opinions think carefully about your response – your body language and the words you use. Again, the chapter 'Talking to children' has more about this. Think about listening in a sympathetic and attentive way. Give children time to express themselves. Don't jump in too soon. Reassure the hesitant children, saying that you value their ideas.

Children need to experience lots of different kinds of questions

Children need to experience lots of different kinds of questions to make them think and to show them how to question and think for themselves. When you pose questions to the children you are guiding them through the debate. You are helping them to think logically through a problem. You are demonstrating what goes on inside your own head when you are asked a difficult question. You are showing them how you need to break the question down into its component parts in order to give a succinct but informative response.

Use questioning as much as you can in your lessons. Try to pose open-ended questions and respond to children's answers with more questions. When you plan your lesson write down the questions you will ask and think about the answers the children will give. Do they allow for further discussion or will the children give a simple yes or no answer?

Children need to know what it is they are evaluating

Children in our primary school classes are moving from a very concrete view of life through to the abstract, ideological thinking of the adult. They need to know exactly what it is they, and you, are looking for when judging or assessing a piece of work or evaluating their behaviour or effort.

Example activities to help children experience different kinds of questions

Hold up a rose at the start of a science lesson in Year 1.

What's this? *A flower.*

How do you know? *I can see it.*

What makes it a flower? *It has leaves and petals and it's pink.*

What else has it got? *A stalk. Roots. Thorns.*

Are all flowers pink? *No, some are different colours.*

How do you know? *I've seen flowers in other colours.*

Can a flower be any colour? *Yes*

How can we find out if that's true? *Look in the garden. Look in books.*

At the start of a history lesson in Year 5 show a picture of a child who is to be evacuated during World War 2.

What do you notice about this child? *He's got a label on. He looks unhappy.*

Why do you say that he looks unhappy? *He's standing looking down at the floor.*

What else do you notice about his face? *Mouth… Eyes…*

How can we find out why he is so unhappy?

Can you think of ways of finding this out?

Is there anyone we could ask about this situation?

You need to provide explicit direction, expressed in positive and concrete terms.

- 'I'm expecting you to concentrate on your use of punctuation in this piece of writing. I shall expect to see full stops and capital letters, and hopefully some commas and speech marks.'

Children need opportunities to practise committing their opinions to the public ear and expressing themselves so that they don't offend others

- 'Make sure that you write only scientific facts in this report. I shall expect to find out a useful piece of information in every sentence.'

- 'When you go outside at playtime I expect you to play without hurting any other child.'

- 'You must not shout out while we are working together. I expect you to put your hand up if you know the answer.'

Tell the children what you are going to be looking for when you mark the piece of work – and don't deviate from this. You are marking a story the child has written. What are you evaluating – spelling, handwriting, structure, use of language, interesting vocabulary? The list is endless. The secret is to match your evaluation to your lesson objective.

- If you have been teaching the children about ways to structure a story so that it is exciting and has a twist to surprise the reader, that is what you should be marking. If the child knows that this is how you are going to evaluate the piece of work then he can put all his effort into that. He knows that he will not be penalised for other errors. He can read through his own work and amend it before handing it to you, knowing what you are both looking for.

Children have a strong sense of justice and will appreciate this approach as being 'fair'. For many children, doing their schoolwork can be like playing a game without knowing the rules. Focusing the task in this way tells the child what the rules for this game are on this occasion.

When you ask the children to give their opinion about, for example, the book they have been reading, provide some clues.

- Tell me about your favourite part.

- What do you think was the point of…?

- Would you read another book by this author?

- What makes you say that?

- Have you read any other historical stories?

Discuss their work with them in small groups. This can be done by a teaching assistant after she has been working with a group of children. She can then feed back the information and opinions to you. Asking questions such as these will guide children's thinking.

- What do you know now that you didn't know at the start of the lesson?

- Is there anything you would like to go over or have more practice at?

- What else would you like to find out about this?

- Was there anything that you found particularly tricky? Was it not explained well?

- How could we have helped you to understand it, do you think?

- Next time we are going to look at…
Do you already know anything about this?

As the children mature and become familiar with the process they will be able to express their responses without you posing the questions.

Children need to be able to recognise their own achievements

In developing self-esteem children pass through a number of stages. The newborn baby doesn't distinguish itself as a separate being. As a toddler the child is beginning to understand that he is a person in his own right. The young child sees himself, and can describe himself, in concrete terms – what he looks like, what he can do. He then starts to compare himself with others and in adolescence can describe himself with reference to feelings, thoughts and ideologies.

Using these stages we can focus the way we help the children in our class to recognise what they have achieved in school. This helps them to build up their self-image. Done sensitively, it will also help to build their self-esteem.

If children learn to recognise all that they have done, track their own development, and share their achievements with pride they will grow in self-respect. With a strong sense of self-esteem, children will have no need to seek attention in antisocial ways.

I can

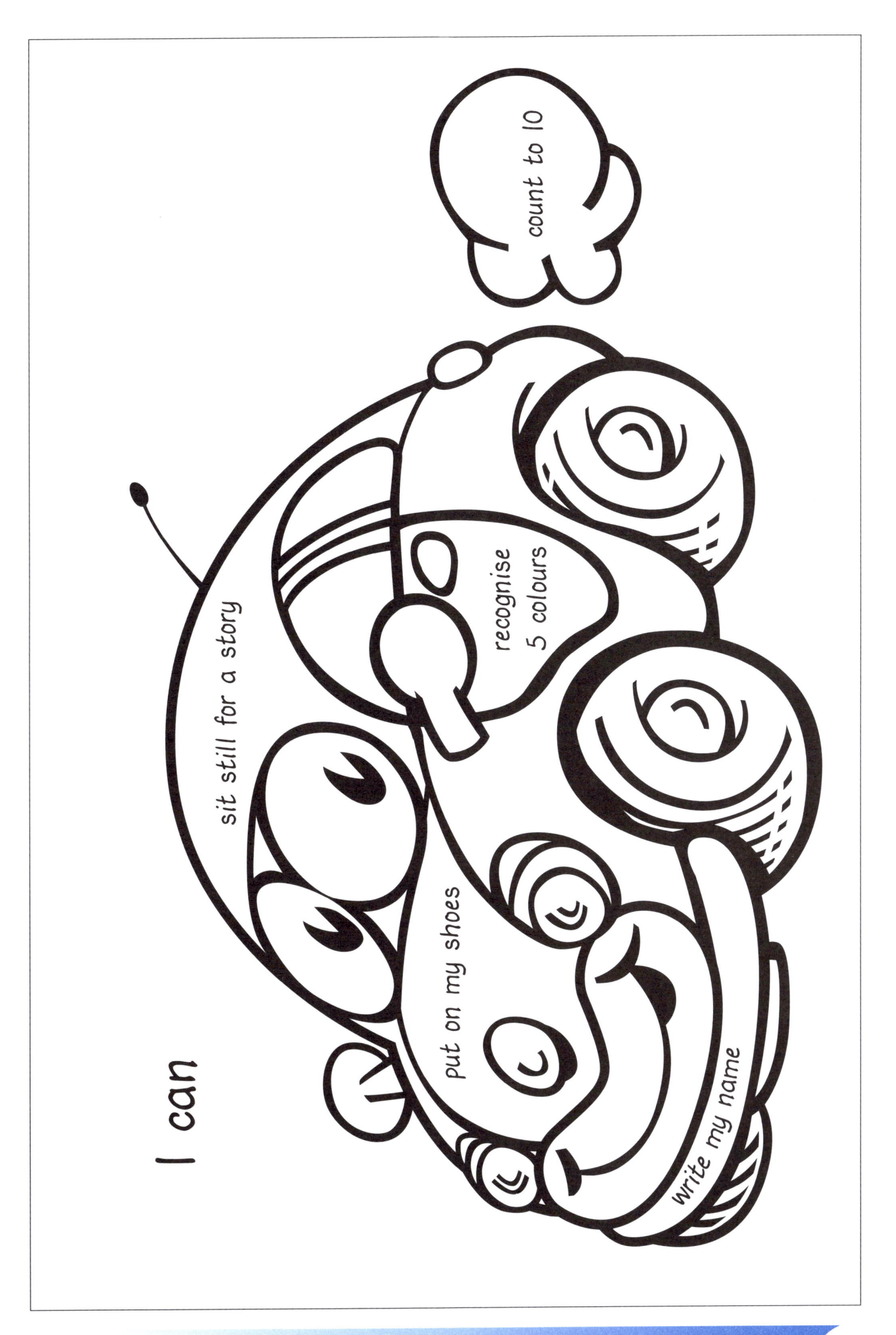

- sit still for a story
- count to 10
- recognise 5 colours
- put on my shoes
- write my name

Things I can do

I can count backwards from 20. 20 19 18 17 16 15 14 13 12 11 10 9 8 7 6 5 4 3 2 1 0	I can estimate up to 10 objects.	I can fold a piece of paper in half.
I can count to 20. 0 1 2 3 4 5 6 7 8 9 10 11 12 13 14 15 16 17 18 19 20	I can count in 10s to 100. 10 20 30 40 50 60 70 80 90 100	I can make a repeating pattern. 123 123 123 2 6 2 6 2
I can make a picture with shapes.	I can count in 2s to 20. 2 4 6 8 10 12 14 16 18 20	I can measure in centimetres.
I can draw a circle, a square, a triangle and a rectangle.	I know odd and even numbers. 1 3 5 7 9 0 2 4 6 8	I can measure in handspans and footprints.

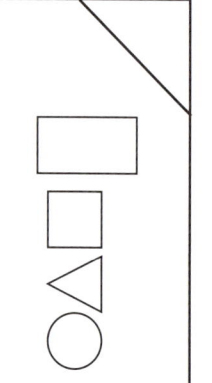

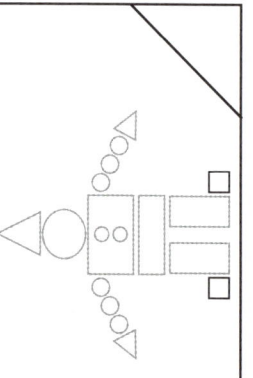

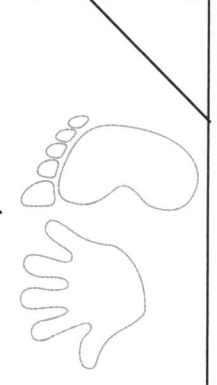

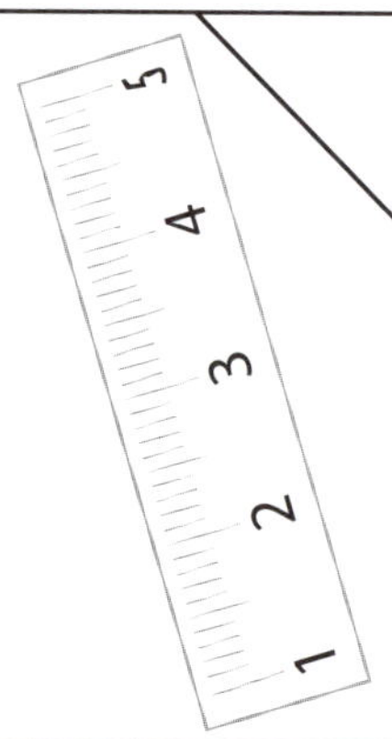

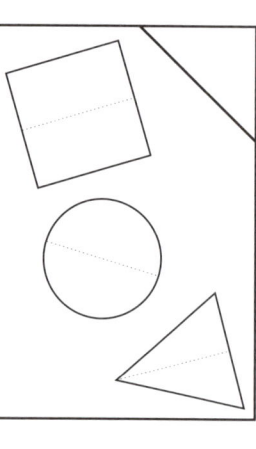

Starting from the Reception class, children can be encouraged to record their own achievements

Using the sheet on p31, children can colour in the individual parts of the picture. When it is complete you can record the completion date against the code for that sheet in your record book. The child can then take the coloured sheet home to share his achievements.

Using the sheet on p32, Things I can do, children can colour in the picture when he and the teacher are sure he can do the task. The date can be placed in the box. Again, record the date when the sheet was completed for your own records and send the sheet home for parents to see.

Targets for literacy and numeracy

Rewrite the literacy and numeracy targets in positive ways.

> 'I can use a capital letter and a full stop in my sentences.'
>
> 'I can write a rhyming poem.'
>
> 'I can count to 100 in tens, both forwards and backwards.'
>
> 'I can say my 7 times table from memory.'

Group the statements according to the levels appropriate for your class, giving each sheet a reference code.

> **In my writing I can**
> - start with a capital letter
> - end with a full stop
> - spell some of the words correctly
> - leave spaces between my words.

Pin them up where the children can see them and help children to determine which sheet they are working towards. At the end of each half-term, work with one group of children at a time, looking through their workbooks and helping them to identify which statements reflect their work. You can record which set of targets they have reached, and the children can see what they have achieved and what they are going to do next. Again, this is tangible evidence to them of all that they have learned.

Make the groups of statements sufficiently challenging or easily manageable in the timescale, dependent on the attitudes and abilities of the children in your class. The important fact is that the children should feel as if they have worked hard and achieved. Too easy, and they will know that they don't need to put much effort into their work. Too hard, and they will become disillusioned and start displaying avoidance tactics.

Targets for IEPs

Break each target down into as many small steps as possible. Try to make one step towards the target for each week of the life of the IEP.

At the end of each week spend time with the child, looking at his work or discussing his behaviour and try to find evidence that he has achieved his target. Cross out the step he has completed, or let him mark it with a highlighter pen, so that he can see what he has done and what he is aiming for next week. This is a task that can be carried out by the child's support worker instead.

Positive reinforcement of success will keep up the momentum of effort and increase the child's self-esteem. In turn, this will reduce the need for the child to avoid work through pretending to lose equipment, sharpening pencils and so on, or to sink into apathy and silly behaviour to distract your attention from his work.

TARGET: To be able to stay on task for the 20 minutes of the independent session of the literacy hour.

WEEK 1	Stay in seat to complete given 5 minute task.	Move quietly to activity in quiet area.
WEEK 2	Stay in seat to complete given 10 minute task.	Move quietly to activity in quiet area.
WEEK 3	Stay in seat to complete given 15 minute task.	Move quietly to activity in quiet area.
WEEK 4	Stay in seat to complete given 15 minute task.	Stay in seat with a choice of quiet activities.
WEEK 5	Stay in seat to complete 2 given tasks, one of 15 minute and one of 5 minute.	
WEEK 6	Stay in seat and complete the same given 20 minute task as other children in the group.	

Children need to learn how to evaluate their work

Allowing for the different stages of development, you can provide processes and systems for children to use as they evaluate their work. This process of evaluation is a useful way of establishing what the children can do. It is also a way of finding out their preferences for different types of activities. It can help you to know where the children need more support so that you can plan for this. Children should feel confident that you will read their responses and react to them appropriately to further their learning.

If you have been providing ways for the children to gain the skills of considering their own thoughts and stating them in helpful and positive ways, this should be a mutually rewarding exercise.

- With younger children, start by talking about what they have learned in that lesson.

  'At the start of this lesson I told you that we were going to write a rhyme together. Did we manage to write our rhyme? Let's read it together. Put your hand up if you like our rhyme. Sam, why do you like it? Who thinks it is funny? Did it make you smile? Who would like to tell us their favourite line? Do you think you could try to write a rhyme yourself tomorrow? Who would like to try to write one with a friend – or a grown-up helper?'

- Younger children can use picture formats to evaluate their response to an activity possibly using the example frames shown. With very young children don't leave this until the end of a complete unit of work. Introduce the idea as an end-of-the-week exercise.

  They can talk about what they have recorded with an adult, who can then add any useful notes, such as 'Joshua was keen to make a model boat but found it very difficult to use the hack-saw as he is left-handed, became frustrated and so didn't enjoy the task'.

- Children could use de Bono's PMI technique, referred to earlier, as an evaluation tool.

  P PLUS: the good things about the work – what I liked doing.

  M MINUS: the bad things about the work – what I didn't like doing.

  I INTERESTING: my favourite things about the work – what I enjoyed doing or learning, something new or fascinating that I learned.

  Children list their opinions under each of these headings. Use it for individual subjects, so that children don't simply write 'Plus – history, Minus – geography, Interesting – science', but

I can

I can nearly

Children can draw something they have learned to do, plus something they are still practising.

My favourite thing this week was	I didn't enjoy
I learned that	I would like to know more about

Children can write or draw something in each box

34 The Positive Behaviour Handbook

ABOUT THE WORK YOU DID

What did you enjoy doing most?

What did you enjoy doing least?

Which piece of work did you find the most difficult?

Why?

What was your best piece of work?

Why?

ABOUT WORKING WITH OTHERS

Did you ask for help when you needed it?

If not, why not?

Did you help anyone with their work?

How?

Do you find it helpful to work with others?

Why?

Do you prefer to work on your own, with one other person, in a small group or do you like it when the whole class is working together with the teacher?

Why?

ABOUT IMPROVING YOUR WORK

Look through your topic book.

Which part of your work has improved the most?

Which part do you need to improve?

How can you do this during the next topic?

Figure 3 Above: End of topic/module of work assessment

LOOK BACK OVER THE WHOLE OF THIS SCHOOL YEAR AS YOU THINK ABOUT YOUR RESPONSES TO THESE HEADINGS

What I have most enjoyed.

What I have least enjoyed.

Things I have done well in.

Things I have got better at.

Things I have found difficult.

Things where I haven't made as much progress as I thought I would.

Ways in which the school could help me to make more progress.

Any other constructive comments you would like to add.

Figure 4 Above: End-of-year self-assessment

think in a more concentrated way about the different types of work they have been doing.

- You can provide the children with a set of questions related to the work they have done.

    What have you learned about…?

    What do you still not understand about…?

    What else would you like to have learned about…?

    Follow this with some factual questions.

    What do we mean by…?

    What is … like in other parts of the world?

    Draw a picture of…

    List 10 things you have learned about…

- Older children will be able to complete a more comprehensive evaluation of their work and their personal responses to it like the ones in Figures 3 and 4. They can be given opportunities to comment on the way they were taught and their preferences for different kinds of approaches.

    Talk through all the sections of the form before the children start to fill it in. Over the year provide opportunities for the children to comment orally or in a written form on these different areas of evaluation. Provide a helper for any child whose writing skills will make it difficult to fill in the form.

    This sheet can be added to the child's record of achievements or other personal school records.

Reading through the comments from the class can be a good way of evaluating your own teaching. You can find out what most appeals to the children and make any changes you feel necessary to your lesson plans, the type of activities you plan and the approaches to learning that you offer the children.

Evaluating behaviour

This chapter has shown how to give children the awareness, the language, the processes and the formats for evaluating – thinking about, reflecting and commenting on – their learning. This is a useful skill for the children to have. Learning to do it well is a non-threatening way of giving them a set of skills which they can also use to consider their behaviour and their responses to others. With these skills they can think about their behaviour and its effects on themselves and on others in the class or the school. Children are able to vocalise their opinions in acceptable ways, to stand their ground in a calm and non-confrontational manner, to see the other person's point of view and so to respond to difficult social situations with self-control.

You may need to include targets for improving behaviour on IEPs or Pastoral Care Plans. You may need to have a class or group discussion with the children about some unacceptable playground behaviour that they've been involved in. You may simply be talking about behaviour in your PSHE lessons. In any of these circumstances you can remind the children about empathy, about constructive criticism and about ways to monitor their steps towards their personal targets.
If behaviour has been a major issue in your class you could include comments on it in your end-of-year assessments.

To sum up

Children with high levels of self-esteem are confident learners, enjoy the respect of their peers and attract friends. Children develop self-esteem in situations which offer positive encouragement and which sensitively foster their growing self-awareness.

We can structure our lessons so that the children can learn about and rehearse skills to increase their self-knowledge and feelings of self-worth.

References and useful additional reading

Bee, H (1989) *The Developing Child (5th Edition)*. New York: Harper & Row.

Bruce, T (1987) *Early Childhood Education*. London: Hodder & Stoughton.

de Bono, E (1992) *Teach Your Child How to Think*. London: Penguin.

Fisher, R (1990) *Teaching Children to Think*. Cheltenham: Stanley Thornes.

Taking responsibility

In this chapter we look at the two sides of taking responsibility.

- Having responsibility.
- Being responsible.

Having responsibility

One of the ten characteristics of an effective school in Rutter (1983) is that it gives real responsibility to the children.

The baby trusts the parent to respond to its needs. The parent fulfils that trust. Most children grow up with this sense of trust in the caring adults around them. Some children are not so fortunate – the adult doesn't respond to the trust the child offers, and the child learns not to trust but to suspect the adult. These early experiences follow the child through his developing years. Some children will not be ready to trust you.

When we give children responsibility in the classroom, we must accompany it with an acknowledgement to the child that we trust him to carry out the action. Be discreet when you check that the job was done. Praise the child so that he knows that you know that he did what you asked of him, without apparently questioning him. Demonstrate to the children that they are worthy of trust.

There are some areas of responsibility that are dependent on whole-school policies. These could include having monitors or prefects around the school corridors, toilet blocks and other public areas, or a formal befriending or buddy system. Others you can implement within your own classroom, at your own discretion and with your particular children in mind.

Who is given responsibility?

Over the course of the year everyone in the class should have responsibility for something. At the beginning of the year, talk to the children about how this will happen. You might have an idea that you will use, or you may be open to suggestions from the children. It will depend on your knowledge of the class. Alternatives include

- going down the register in age or alphabetical order
- choosing an equal number of boys and girls at a time
- asking children to sign up to particular roles and then listing the volunteers and working down the list.

How long will they be in post?

For the very youngest children this may be only one day – 'Today Mary is going to give out the pencil pots.' It can become a week, a half-term or a whole term. Some areas of responsibility may depend on children gaining some skills, such as in the more formal buddy scheme. Their responsibilities will then be ongoing. Some of the more mundane classroom roles can become tedious and it is more effective to change the roles at frequent intervals before apathy and boredom set in than to risk the responsibility becoming onerous. Change the names each week so that everyone has turns at different roles over the year.

What will they be called?

You may be in a school with a system of monitors or prefects already in place. It may be expected that you will use these terms in your classroom. It may be that you have freedom to choose. Again, this is something you can discuss with the children, especially older ones, and find out what they prefer. They must be allowed to keep their street cred!

Options include

- monitors
- prefects
- helpers.

How will they be identified?

You will need to have a display in the room to remind everyone who is responsible for what this week. You may also choose to provide a badge of some kind for the children to wear. Keep these in school and hand them out each morning, or you could lose many of them to the washing machine and the dog.

Wall charts/rotas

For young children

Make a large card chart. On the left-hand side list the 'jobs'. On the right-hand side you can either cut vertical slits, two per line, into which you can tuck the ends of name cards. Or you can attach two small lengths of elastic, or treasury tags, vertically for holding the ends of the name cards.

Make one card for each child in the class and keep them in a box next to the chart. Each week place last week's name cards at the back of the box and take this week's from the front of the box. This is an easy and systematic way to give every child a fair chance. If someone is absent you can leave their card at the front ready for next week.

For older children

Produce a chart on the computer, with interesting graphics and colours. Change the names and reprint when you change areas of responsibility around. This could be a task in your ICT work.

Commercially produced charts

These are available but you will have to look carefully at what is on offer. Does it include all the responsibilities that you are planning to delegate? Does it allow you to have two children for each job, if that would be helpful in your classroom? Is it easy to use or will it soon be consigned to the back of the cupboard?

Badges

Catalogues will offer badges with the word 'monitor' and so on. You can also buy plain coloured badges which will simply indicate that this person is helping out in some way. Or you could produce your own with a special design on them.

An alternative is to use a small length of ribbon looped and pinned in place. Think carefully about the colour, especially if boys or older children are expected to wear them. Choose your school colours for least argument.

You may think it unnecessary to have any badges at all and prefer to rely on the chart for reference.

What are the benefits of being a responsible person in the classroom?

You can include benefits as part of the reward for taking on this responsibility. If you have a small seating area such as a bench in your classroom, then the children who are monitors can sit on this during story time or at registration, whilst the others sit on the floor. The monitors can come into the classroom before the start of school to carry out their tasks if this is appropriate and you can be in there with them.

The unseen benefit is all about raising self-esteem. It is part of the process of making children feel secure about themselves. It is a way of giving them attention for socially supportive acts. It gives everyone an equal chance to help out.

Children will feel important, knowing that you trust them and that the other children are depending on them for something. Some children will take this in their stride. For other children this can be a major boost to their self-confidence and heighten their sense of worth within the community of the classroom. For a child who is new to the school, a routine task such as sharpening pencils can give him an anchor at a time when he may be feeling very vulnerable.

What if a child abuses his position?

This is an issue that should be discussed with the class as a whole at the start of the year. Work out the ground rules together. It can be approached in the same way as setting out the classroom rules (see the chapter 'Day one: rules and routines').

Agree the sanctions that will follow any breaking of trust. These might include

- giving up his position immediately
- receiving one warning, then losing his position if there is a repeat offence.

The child should still be given a job to do next time his turn comes up.

What if the child asks to give up the responsibility?

Consider making some tasks last for shorter periods of time and allocate these to children who you know to have a short concentration time.

It's not a good idea to make a child continue in the job if he is determined that he doesn't want it or is unhappy and uncomfortable doing it. The job won't get done. You can end up dealing with a child who is unhappy or even angry over something which is of secondary importance to his work. First, try persuasion. See if you can agree a compromise –

'If you can just do it until the end of the week it would be better for us all. Then you can give it up.' If this is not agreed, accept his resignation but let him know that he will still be considered next time you are sharing out the responsibilities.

What sort of responsibilities should children be given?

Infants

At this age children will be happy to take responsibility for any of the mundane jobs in the classroom. The following tasks are well within their capabilities and achievements are tangible.

- Check that all the pencils and crayons are in the right pots at the end of the morning and afternoon sessions.
- Sharpen pencils and crayons.
- Give out exercise books or paper.
- Collect in books.
- Give out rulers, counters, alphabet sheets and so on.
- Feed the fish.
- Make sure that the home corner is tidy.
- Make sure that there are no coats left in the cloakroom at the end of the day.

Juniors

Many junior age children will still be happy to take on the roles described for the infants, but some will be ready for tasks which involve supporting other children.

- Helping the Reception children at lunchtime. Sitting with them and helping them to open yogurt pots, crisp packets and so on.
- Reading with younger children at prearranged times. Sharing their book and keeping their reading record up to date.
- Acting as befrienders to new children in their own class, until they have made their own friends.
- Looking after the Reception children on the playground for the first few days or until they are settled. Playing with them, helping them with coats, taking them to adult supervisors if they are hurt or upset, showing them where the toilets are and waiting to show them the way back to the playground.
- Showing visitors around the school. Some schools have this as a whole-school policy and

> The unseen benefit is all about raising self-esteem

your children may need to be excused to go and do this. You can also ask them to show new children around the school, introducing them to the staff and the other classes, and showing them where to find the toilets, the library, the office and so on.

What skills will the children need to carry out these tasks?

Showing visitors around

Talk with the whole class about how you expect them to do this.

- What route will they follow?
- How will they enter busy classes?
- When should they not enter?
- How do you introduce people?

There are many high level social skills to be practised as children undertake this activity.

Befriending other children

- Discuss the limits of what the children should do.
- Talk about the purpose – to settle the children in, not to dominate them or prevent them from making their own friends.
- Discuss the need to be on hand to help, but not to overwhelm the child.
- Talk about what they will do if the child doesn't want to be helped in this way – how to stay at a distance but keep an eye on the child to make sure that he is alright.
- When should they go to you or to the child's teacher to explain something that happened? Perhaps the child was crying, or another child rejected him. Perhaps he was hurting other children.

In schools where a formal buddy system is in place children are trained to respond to the needs of the other children, and in how to intervene in disagreements. Without such a system and training children should not be expected to take this on. Make sure that the children know what is expected of them and the limits of what they are allowed to do when acting as befrienders.

> In addition to giving children responsibilities you also need to think about enabling children to be responsible

Being responsible

In addition to giving children responsibilities you also need to think about enabling children to be responsible. This involves being able to make informed choices about their actions and their reactions to people and events. Much of this will occur within lessons you plan for PSHE and citizenship.

Children need to be able to make choices

Making a choice involves

- listening to both sides of an argument
- thinking about the repercussions of choosing either side
- using this information to make a choice.

In its simplest form children might be choosing jam or honey on their toast.

- 'I like jam. I don't like honey. I'll have jam.'
- 'I like jam and I like honey. Today I think I'll have honey and I'll have jam tomorrow.'
- 'I can't decide so I'll have one piece of toast with jam and the other piece of toast with honey.'

The answer is neither right nor wrong, nor does it actually matter.

When it comes to making a choice that crops up on a regular basis, such as whether to do your homework or not, the decision has repercussions that the child already knows about.

- 'If I do my homework straightaway I can get out to play before it gets dark and Mum calls me in.'
- 'If I don't do my homework tonight I could do it before I go to school, but last time I tried that I slept in and didn't have time to do it properly and Miss was not too pleased.'
- 'If I don't do it Mum will go on at me, like she did last week. She said I would be in big trouble if I didn't do it properly this week and I want her in a good mood when I ask if I can go to the football with Jamie. I think I'd better just do it.'

Children can use their experiences to make a decision.

At other times children will be facing a decision that they have never faced before. They will need to draw on their experiences, their knowledge of people and how they could react, and of situations

The Positive Behaviour Handbook

that could occur, to work out what the result of any choice might be.

In PSHE lessons children can talk about these possibilities and learn about some of the options open to them. They can think about the repercussions of different responses they could make. They may be put under peer pressure to join in activities which hurt or upset other children. They may be asked to try drugs or be offered cigarettes or alcohol. They can be threatened by others or bullied systematically. We can't protect our children every minute of every day, but we can equip them with the life skills to make informed choices and deal with these situations.

Likes and dislikes

The youngest children can start with making choices based on things they like and things they dislike. They can be shown that others may make different decisions but that these are equally acceptable. You can play games with picture cards.

- Choose three things that you like and three that you dislike from these ten pictures.
- What about the four that are left?
- What if you had to put one of them back?
- Why did you choose this one?
- Has your friend chosen the same ones as you?
- Now work with your friend and do the same exercise together.
- What happens – how can you sort out any differences of opinion?

Play the game with pictures of fruit, cars, toys and so on. The level of the discussion can be extended by, for example, including pictures of faces showing different emotions.

Fair and unfair

Describe a scenario and offer two endings. Children can decide whether the endings are fair or unfair. 'Why do you think that? What if the child in the story was an adult, then would it be fair?'

- 'Polly had to go to the shop for her mum. She had a two-pound coin. On the way home she fell over and dropped the coin and it rolled down the drain. When she got home her mum

    a) told her off for being careless and not looking where she was going

    b) gave her a cuddle because she was crying and then put a plaster on her cut knee.'

- 'Samir was out playing football with his friend Chris. They took their coats off and put them over the fence at the side of the field. When they went back for them they realised that the fence had just been painted and there was sticky black paint down both of their coats. Samir's mum was

    a) was very cross and said that Samir would have to save up his pocket money to pay for the cleaning

    b) said that it wasn't his fault as people shouldn't paint fences without putting up a notice to let passers-by know that the paint was wet.'

Right or wrong

Provide the children with a scenario, then divide them into small groups and ask each group to come up with a two-minute drama to show the scenario when the characters make the 'right' choice and another to show what happens when the characters make the 'wrong' choice.

- 'Three friends are on their way to school. A young man is standing on the street corner. As they pass him he calls them over and takes a small packet out of his pocket. What should they do?'

- 'Three friends are playing football in the park when they see a man they've never seen before standing near the gates watching a child who is on her own. The man walks towards her and offers her some sweets. What will the friends do?'

Talk to the groups as they work out their dramas. It may not be feasible to watch every group perform at the end of the session, depending on the number of groups you have. As an alternative you could brainstorm their responses and categorise them – interfere, call for help, ignore, keep watching, find out the facts before you jump to conclusions.

You could discuss the dangers of making the wrong choice, however well-intentioned you were. You can make children aware of the need to get the whole picture and not just jump to conclusions. The young man might have been calling you over to ask the time or the way, while getting himself a sweet from his pocket. He could have been a drug dealer. The man in the park might have been the child's father or grandfather, or he may have been a complete stranger tempting her to go away with him. They could be putting themselves in danger by interfering personally.

It is important for children to learn that not all situations offer a clear-cut choice. The answer might not be good or bad, right or wrong. Most decisions we make in life are something of a compromise. Children gradually learn this important lesson and can face up to issues of conflict, think through the options open to them and arrive at a decision.

To sum up

Giving responsibility means giving trust. Children who feel trusted will begin to have confidence in their own ability to make a valued contribution to society. They can then start to develop their own ethos of care for their environment and for their fellow human beings.

References

Rutter, M (1983) School effects on pupil progress: Research findings and policy implications. *Child Development* 54, 1–29

> Children who feel trusted will begin to have confidence in their own ability to make a valued contribution to society

SECTION THREE

Rewards, sanctions and expectations

We all repeat behaviours that are rewarded. For many children this reward is adult attention. It is in the hands of teachers whether they reward positive behaviour by paying attention to the child who is working and behaving well, or whether they respond to negative behaviour by giving the children lots of time and attention when they are unruly or disruptive in any way. It makes sense to continually reinforce children's positive behaviour in the classroom. This will have a greater and longer-lasting effect on improving the learning environment for the children than the constant identification and punishment of negative behaviour, which for many children is the only way they know of gaining the attention that they crave.

In this section we look at the different ways in which you can reward the children in your class as they conform to the rules and expectations of the community of the class. There is also advice on agreeing and using sanctions in a positive way, to reinforce your expectations of the children, not merely as punishments. Children need help to learn what is expected of them, and support as they practise these new skills.

Rewards

Think about the kinds of behaviours of others that motivate and reward us, as adults, in our work in school. They probably include informal rewards such as people valuing our opinions by seeking them out, expressing gratitude for all the effort we've put into organising something like a school trip, and trusting us to make decisions and take responsibility for areas of the school community. Then there are the more formal rewards, such as recognition that we're ready for the next step on the career ladder, or a pay increase. Someone might also really make you feel good by giving you a special treat in recognition of how much effort you've put into helping them or making something work.

Children are no different. They also respond to these informal and formal rewards.

What are rewards?

It's important to recognise the many different types of rewards that you can make use of and the way you can categorise these for your own use.

For example, you can distinguish between *informal* rewards, such as smiling or verbal praise and *formal* rewards, such as house point systems and certificates.

Some people choose to refer to the former as *encouragement* rather than informal rewards, and the latter as *incentives* rather than formal rewards. In this chapter we use the terms interchangeably, as both are widely used.

Encouragement or informal rewards

The focus is on the effort that the child is putting in. So, for example, they would include remarks such as 'You thought hard about that – well done', or 'I can see you're considering Sam's opinion carefully – well done', or a thumbs up and a smile as a child offers a response.

Incentives or formal rewards

These focus on a sense of having achieved something specific. They are often a more public form of praise and must be balanced with encouragement and informal rewards to be of real use.

Why use rewards?

There are lots of good reasons for using rewards. A raft of publications before and especially since the Elton Report Discipline in Schools (1989) provides the theoretical justification for them. However, experienced teachers know from their own practice that rewards

- help to nurture positive relationships – the cornerstone of effective behaviour management – and the promotion of positive behaviour
- help to make the school experience a happy and positive one
- encourage children to repeat desired behaviours
- encourage other children to demonstrate desired behaviours
- contribute to the development of the children's self-esteem and confidence, positively affecting their social and academic achievements
- help build working relationships with parents and carers.

All teachers have slightly different teaching styles and so encouragement and informal rewards will differ slightly from class to class. However, it is important that there is a whole-school agreement on the incentives and, in particular, formal rewards given, to ensure consistency throughout the school in this often public and sometimes competitive form of rewarding a child's positive behaviour. Some teachers have reservations about some forms of rewards, so staff must agree their approach.

Using rewards

It's easy for teachers to feel demoralised by reward systems, because they seem difficult to use fairly and can become yet another thing to manage and organise in a busy primary classroom. The good news is that the most effective, but overlooked, reward systems are often the simplest – they are the little things that you can do as you teach which encourage children, reward their efforts and so build their self-esteem and confidence. Remember that for children the ultimate reward is

- to succeed at what they are trying to do
- to have others recognise that success
- to experience the positive feeling that success brings.

Your children's self-esteem determines the extent to which they will realise their potential. Protecting and nurturing self-esteem is central to all the rewards, sanctions and other behaviour management strategies you use. There may be times when certain children may benefit from individual behaviour charts or diaries, but these are the exception, not the rule. Your own individual efforts – informal rewards – need to be supported by wider, whole-school formal rewards such as good-news letters and certificates. You may wish to use certificates and stickers of your own in class in addition to the formal systems in place in your school. However, the encouraging informal rewards listed in this chapter are the crucial building blocks of any reward system and to a large extent are the most important reward system you can provide.

Informal rewards

Consider how aware you are of intentionally using the following strategies for informal rewards.

- Smiling and nodding in encouragement.
- Thumbs up.
- Verbal praise.
- Using your voice tone to show delight, surprise or appreciation.
- Showing approval by saying something positive and encouraging or writing it on a book or piece of work, combining an appropriate tone with words that make it clear you're pleased or impressed.

    'That's wonderful – look at X…', 'You've really got it – well done!'

- Showing gratitude to a child, either through a private word of appreciation – more suitable for some older children or initially with those whose self-esteem is very low – or a public acknowledgement in which the child is able to demonstrate their achievement to an audience.
- Catching children being good and letting them know you've noticed their excellent work (see later on in this chapter and 'Catch them being good!' on p52).
- Showing children that you trust them, for example by giving them responsibilities which they may be surprised at, without doubting that they'll manage the job. Never say you are looking round the class for a sensible, intelligent or trustworthy child. All children must be encouraged to think that you can see these qualities in them, rather than getting the message that you're working to a deficit model – a danger which easily becomes reality. You will no doubt be thinking about who you can trust for the job, but the message to the children is 'Oh, I'm spoilt for choice – I've never had a class full of such sensible, caring children as all of you'.

> The good news is that the most effective, but overlooked, reward systems are often the simplest

- Demonstrating that the children's contributions and opinions on a range of issues are important by seeking them out. Ask for their ideas on what would make a good display, how to improve wet playtimes and so on, and show that you are listening to them by taking up one or two suggestions, explaining why these suggestions have been chosen and not others. Answer all contributions sensitively, regardless of their value and help a child not to lose face by taking kindly inappropriate suggestions or answers which were well meant. Extend work on setting class rules by continuing to involve children in making decisions on personal, class and school issues.

- Allowing children to share achievements with other people. For example, do send children to the head, deputy, KS2 leader, etc. – not for bad behaviour, but to show them something fantastic that's just been achieved.

    - Send a sticky note – 'I know you'll love this drawing of Ben's', 'Look at the brilliant use of adjectives in Adam's piece of writing', 'Alison's been really helpful to her friends this afternoon' – to help direct your colleague's attention.

    - Send the child with a verbal message.

    - Simply ask the child to show the work to another teacher, after expressing your own response to it.

    This needs to be agreed as a strategy that can be used with staff around the school so that any generally inconvenient times (such as the beginning of whole-class sessions) can be avoided. Alternatively, work with one colleague who understands what you're trying to achieve and who will help reinforce your message.

With more difficult children, think about whether there is one member of staff to whom they relate particularly well and make her the person with whom they can share their successes. If a child has developed a pattern of being sent to the headteacher for poor behaviour, make her the person to whom evidence of success can be shown.

- Telling someone else about the child's achievements within the child's hearing.

- Telling colleagues and asking them to congratulate the child if they get the opportunity.

- Asking to see the child's parents or carers to surprise them with the good news (as long as your parents know that this is part of your strategy)!

- Displaying and publishing the children's work.

- Reading something to the class (perhaps without identifying the child) and asking others to say something positive about it.

- Encouraging children to show work they are proud of during whole-class times such as the end of the day or during circletime.

- Encouraging children to praise each other.

- Marking work positively, with constructive verbal and written comments that encourage and motivate the child.

Formal rewards

The following are some strategies for formal rewards or incentives. Consider how many of these you use.

- A daily or weekly class celebration time

    This is best timetabled at a specific point in the day/week and should follow a pattern. It may involve the presentation of stickers or certificates. It needs to be carefully planned and managed to prevent children from feeling left out, which can happen to those in the middle range of a class who are neither shining academically nor being heavily focused on to improve their behaviour. This can be demotivating and may even lead to such children feeling resentful.

- A special day for each child

    This could involve a badge and a certificate designed by some of the class. Other class members can write a positive statement about the child on the certificate. 'Special days' can involve privileges and responsibilities and be earned by an anonymous vote from the class, or be awarded by the teacher. Careful management is again required, to prevent children from missing out or the system taking on a tokenistic quality, with children deciding that once the day has been awarded to them, it won't happen again until everyone else in the class has had a turn. The notion of what a special day is, how it is awarded and how everyone in the class community can contribute to the experience is something that must be fully explored in PSHE/circletimes.

- Good news letters or postcards sent home in the post

  A very welcome piece of post amongst the bills! There is more advice on this in the chapter 'Writing to parents'.

- Good news telephone calls home

  Useful for parents who are not often seen at school, with whom you are trying to develop a working relationship.

- A range of certificates to take home or display in class

  For example, 'Star of the week', 'Good work', an 'ME' award – Maximum Effort.

- Stickers and point systems

  These are the rewards that can cause the most consternation among teachers, children and parents – yet they are widely used and can be successful if very carefully planned and managed.

  – House points

    This involves the children being in different houses, within the class, year or whole school. House points can be awarded by any staff member and recorded on a public chart in the classroom, either by the child or the adult. At the end of the week or half-term the points are added up and announced in assembly. At the end of the half-term, term or year there is some kind of ceremony, usually involving a trophy and coloured ribbons, in which the captain and vice-captain of the winning house accept the trophy on behalf of the house and it is put on public display. Points towards the trophy are also earned at events such as sports day.

    This system involves peer pressure. It is not universally liked or thought to be motivating to children. However, if it is in use in your school, make the most of it by encouraging the children to be a part of the collective effort towards the success of their house. Be sure to award points for a range of social, learning and collaborative skills and attitudes, as well as for academic achievements. Keep a close eye on who is earning what and whether some children are showing no interest or being overlooked.

  – Stickers

    There is an enormous range of colourful, attractive stickers available, all of which are well liked by children. The problem lies in ensuring their consistent use, and in their impact being lessened by overuse. Stickers can be made into badges. They are an instant reward which can be recognised by others for the rest of the day, often resulting in even more praise for the child wearing the sticker.

  – Stamps

    Ink stamps in a child's workbooks are another form of sticker, but a more private way of encouraging him.

- Special assemblies

  Whole-school good work and celebration assemblies are usually very popular, with parents and carers being invited to attend this public acknowledgement of a child's efforts and achievements. Make sure that all children have the opportunity to take part and be sensitive to those for whom it can be a difficult experience. Choose a range of things to celebrate.

- Good Work and Thank You books

  Again, shared in assembly, these books are kept in a public place and can be written in by any adult, so that a child can receive public praise that he may not expect at a good work assembly. Alternatively, the book may be sited in an area where all children can access it and also contribute thanks and positive messages to other children or staff.

> In a Good Work or Thank You book, a child can receive public praise that he may not be expecting

The Positive Behaviour Handbook

- **Child-specific reward programmes**
  - Drawn up alongside a child's behaviour targets, these require careful consideration and close monitoring and are not to be used lightly, as without the appropriate amount of effort they often do not achieve their aim and contribute to a sense of failure. However, if well managed they give a child tangible evidence of his progress and provide the motivation to keep working at set behaviour targets.

- **Other forms of public praise**
  - Notice boards that record academic and social achievements, sited in a public place such as the entrance hall.
  - Displays outside the classroom that show children's work and their names.

With both of these it is important to be sensitive to the impact that such public praise may have on the children concerned.

What makes rewards work?

Remember that rewards must genuinely motivate a child, be genuinely earned by the child and be sincerely given by the teacher. If they lose their meaning they will cease to have effect.

Some children with very low self-esteem find it difficult to accept encouragement and rewards. They find it very difficult to accept that you genuinely value their work and efforts and are easily embarrassed if praised in front of others. Always encourage these children, even if they seem to try to reject it. Keep it short, succinct and focused on the effort the child has put in, and initially keep it quiet and private. As confidence and self-esteem grow, the child will begin to be able to accept low-key public acknowledgements.

A framework

To be effective, rewards need to be securely established within a framework of rules, routines and class values that encourage children to respect each other's rights and to take responsibility for their own actions. The framework must be consistently adhered to.

Working with parents

Rewards need to be understood and supported by parents. Parents can only do this if they understand your approach, so include and involve them as much as possible. There should be general information for all parents and specific information for those whose children are receiving extra attention from you concerning their behaviour.

Many parents are used to being contacted only when something has gone wrong. It can have a powerful and positive effect on a child's motivation and the parents' support of the child if they are suddenly contacted about good behaviour. This can be informal – a few words at the end of school, such as 'I just wanted to let you know how hard Sam has worked today at being a good friend/concentrating on his work' or a telephone call to those parents who are not seen very often at school. Or it can be more formal, for example the use of a Good news letter or postcard designed by the school and sent by post to create a feel-good factor for parents and child.

Making sure that the rewards are genuinely motivating the children

As obvious as it sounds, you need to be sure that the rewards you use are genuinely motivating the children. If the house-point or 'Star of the week' systems have lost their impact, which could happen for a variety of reasons, change them. Opportunities for regularly speaking and listening together, such as circletimes, will provide information for you on the perspectives of the children in your class. As you get to know them better you will learn more about what motivates them. You'll also have the chance to ask them why it is that the other systems are no longer popular. Children's opinions are invariably illuminating – take the time to seek them out and listen to them.

Children who have individualised behaviour programmes will probably need something very particular to motivate them. The only way to find this out is to get to know the child. It may be something as unlikely as having a time to sing to the class, helping younger children in another class or having responsibility for a specific job in the class.

Something else to consider is the age and maturity of the children. The different approaches chosen must be appropriate for the developmental stage of the children, particularly their social and emotional development.

Teachers have limitless obligations and it's easy to forget or fall out of the habit of using a range of rewards, particularly with those parents who are difficult to involve in the process or those children who seem not to respond. Teachers can and do make a very real difference to children's attitudes to learning, their attitude to themselves and others and to their achievements, both in and outside school. Therefore, be tenacious in your efforts – never give up. All children fundamentally want to succeed, to be seen to succeed, to be liked and to feel happy in their time at school. This sometimes seems not to be the case, but effective teachers get to know their children well enough to understand how to meet their needs and how to help them move towards positive behaviour patterns.

Review the system of rewards used in your class and the way in which it is managed. Remember that even rewards can be threatening and induce anxiety in children – which in itself blocks learning – if they are not managed fairly and consistently.

Reflecting on your own practice

If possible, ask a colleague or friend to make a video recording of your teaching. It's an invaluable experience in your professional development. Don't act to the camera – forget about it if you can. Analyse the tape for the balance of positive and negative messages you give children as you interact with them, looking at body language, language chosen, intonation and actions.

Many teachers are surprised at the relatively small amount of positive feedback they project compared to negative. There are lots of reasons for this, but having identified it as a possible area for professional development, you can set about learning new habits for responding to the children. Repeat the recording after a while, observing the same areas and also the children's reactions to you.

At the beginning of each day, look forward positively to the learning ahead. The end of the day should be a time for reflection on what has been learned and experienced during the school day and to consolidate the values you are promoting. This can include a celebration of how you worked through any difficult things that happened, and should leave children with a sense of achievement and responsibility for what you have all learned from the day's events. The sense of being a valued member of a class community is rewarding and motivating in itself.

Remember that what you are aiming for is children who are able to take responsibility for their own behaviour – motivated learners with the degree of self-esteem and self-confidence that enables them to take risks in their learning. Your use of rewards is one tool in your pursuit of this aim, in which the extrinsic motivations you employ lead children to develop their own intrinsic motivation – interest and fulfilment in their pursuit of learning.

References

Elton Report (1989) *Discipline in Schools, Report of the Committee of Inquiries*. London: HMSO.

Catch them being good!

Think of the many opportunities to show children you've noticed their positive behaviour in

- coming into the room quietly
- being kind
- showing enthusiasm
- carrying out a classroom job responsibly
- offering help without being asked
- staying on task
- telling the truth
- rising to a new challenge
- behaving courteously to visitors to the school
- doing extra research outside school
- taking part in school clubs and events
- showing a positive attitude
- making their best effort
- taking part in activities in the wider community
- taking part in a group activity
- showing creativity
- keeping busy when work is finished
- taking turns
- working cooperatively with a helper or teaching assistant
- being a good friend
- being punctual
- getting on with what they know they should be doing
- being a good, active listener in circletime
- making a smooth transition between activities
- following directions
- showing good manners, eg. saying please and thank you
- listening carefully
- helping someone
- bringing all the things they need, eg. PE kit
- handing in homework on time
- being a good audience at a performance
- settling to their work quickly
- asking questions when they're not sure what to do
- being calm before and during a stressful time (eg. a formal test) or a problem situation (eg. a disagreement)
- taking part in a class discussion
- walking sensibly
- working cooperatively
- taking part in a performance in class or school hall
- putting resources away without being asked
- working hard at something
- sharing their school experiences with their parents
- making a new friend
- sharing
- being sensitive to others' feelings
- befriending a new class member
- learning a new skill
- helping a younger or less able person to learn a new skill
- using school resources appropriately and carefully
- returning borrowed books or materials
- helping someone to sort out a problem, eg. an argument
- showing respect for other people's views in a debate
- returning school letters, etc. on time.

There are lots more! The more you seek out positive behaviour, the more you find.

Sanctions

Schools need to balance their rewards with an agreed hierarchy of sanctions. However, resorting to sanctions too quickly will leave teachers with nowhere else to go. They should only be used in conjunction with a wide range of classroom management strategies and rewards. Sanctions discourage inappropriate behaviour, but they do not teach new, more appropriate behaviours, so they must not be overused or relied upon too heavily.

It is important for teachers to remember the following.

- Children are likely to keep misbehaving if that's when they get most attention.
- Children who no longer feel motivated to conform to the ethos and values of the school are often those who have become totally disaffected – because they have become desensitised to teachers telling them off and have very low self-esteem. They are often victims of a cycle of criticism.

Reminders

Teachers need to use a range of skills to prevent them moving into sanctions inappropriately. Aim for a reminder of the rule to be given first – the fairness of this can be agreed in discussion with children. If teachers make the point that they also forget things sometimes, and that it's only fair to be reminded of a rule before someone gets a little more serious about it, the children will usually respond. The teacher can then give them responsibility for choosing to keep or break a rule.

Reminders may include verbal messages or non-verbal ones, such as hand signals which can be agreed with the class in an enjoyable code-making discussion. Hand signals have the advantage of allowing a teacher to communicate with a child without interrupting the flow of their conversation with others. Hand signals are particularly useful for

- sit up
- sit down
- turn round
- put the chair legs on the floor
- stop what you are doing
- listen carefully
- look carefully

and don't forget… thumbs up and a smile!

Always provide a chance for a child to demonstrate the positive behaviour you are promoting before moving towards sanctions. Doing this in a friendly, firm way, which implies your complete confidence that the child has simply forgotten and will keep to the agreed rules, provides everyone with the chance to avoid confrontation and for the child to save face in front of his peer group. Everything that is done in promoting positive behaviour – particularly in the application of sanctions – needs to have at its core a commitment to protecting and nurturing a child's self-esteem.

Consistency

Beyond reminders, sanctions need to be organised in a hierarchy and agreed throughout the school. Consistent use of sanctions throughout the school is essential. A typical hierarchy would be as follows.

- A private reminder.
- A warning of the sanction that will follow if the poor behaviour continues. This needs to be presented as the child choosing whether to keep to the agreed rules or experience the sanction.
- Temporary isolation of the child within the classroom.
- Temporary isolation of the child from the classroom – this and the previous point can also be used as a positive support strategy by the child if used as time out within an area that includes prompts that encourage the child to think about what's gone wrong and how to move forward.
- Informing or asking to see parents.
- Temporary exclusion of the child from the classroom.
- Temporary exclusion of the child from the school at certain times, eg. lunchtime.
- Temporary or permanent exclusion from school.

Other sanctions, perhaps directly related to the misdemeanour (for instance cleaning the graffiti off the wall), referring the child to a more senior member of staff, or the loss of a privilege, may occur within such a hierarchy.

Implementation

The most damaging attitude when working towards improving behaviour in school is that of teachers not believing that children can change

Sanctions must be applied consistently, firmly, fairly and without confrontation.

If sanctions are agreed during the establishment phase of the year, the children will understand the need for them and respect their use. If they are inconsistently applied it will cause difficulties. Deliberately ignoring certain infringements of rules is an area where teachers have to be very analytical and be sure that their actions will lead to the behaviour they are seeking.

Once a sanction has been implemented, the child needs to be helped to see that the matter is over, everyone is looking forward, and he or she has a fresh start. As a teacher, you need to quickly refocus on the work in hand and find an early opportunity to praise the child for his efforts or achievements, so moving your joint focus back to the child's progress.

It is vital that teachers remain emotionally neutral when giving sanctions and remember that they are role models. This isn't always easy, but raising your voice and getting annoyed will give the message that it is alright to do this if you need to get a point across, which is not the message you are trying to promote. To maintain a focus on promoting positive behaviour when applying a sanction, teachers need to model respect.

They can do this by

- keeping the focus on the behaviour
- applying the sanction privately, rather than in public
- calmly keeping the focus on the sanction which has been 'chosen' by the child without adding negative messages, so letting the experience of the sanction carry the teaching point
- moving forward after the sanction has been imposed – encouraging the child by positively focusing on aspects of his work and reinforcing the message that the misdemeanour is behind him.

Working towards keeping to the rules

Children need teachers to help them keep to the rules by creating the conditions for them to demonstrate positive behaviour, praising them for it and acknowledging the efforts that are being made. Praise should always outweigh reprimand. Teachers can help in the following ways.

- Remind children about the rules by celebrating them when they are being kept.

- Use strategies such as signals that indicate a warning to a child when a reminder has been ignored, and let him know the behaviour has been noted, but that do not interrupt the flow of teaching and do not embarrass the child or risk a confrontation. Examples of this include eye contact, privately understood signals with individual children, the use of hand signals that allow the teacher to continue teaching, and phrases such as 'We're just waiting for three children now'. The anonymity of this phrase gives children a chance to behave in the expected way without being confronted.

- Encourage children's participation by responding positively to children's contributions (see chapter 4 'Talking to children').

- Ensure that sanctions are not 'threatened', but occur naturally as part of the class agreement on how it functions without reverting to confrontations.

- Ensure that any behaviour that is deliberately ignored is addressed privately with a child.

- Ensure that a stated course of action is followed up.

- Help children to save face in front of others, to avoid an escalation of poor behaviour.

- Most importantly, ensure that the child understands from your actions that it is the behaviour that you do not like, not him. If a

Positive behaviour checklist

From what has been covered so far in this book we can draw up a checklist of the key principles of promoting positive behaviour.

- ❏ Consistency.
- ❏ An explicit focus on the values that build a strong class community.
- ❏ Establishing the 4 Rs – rules, rights, responsibilities and routines – and reinforcing these throughout the year.
- ❏ The consistent use of sanctions and rewards.
- ❏ Positive relationships.
- ❏ A commitment to maximising children's self-esteem and confidence.
- ❏ Mutual respect.
- ❏ Motivated learners and teachers.
- ❏ High expectations.
- ❏ A sense of humour.

The 'criticism trap'

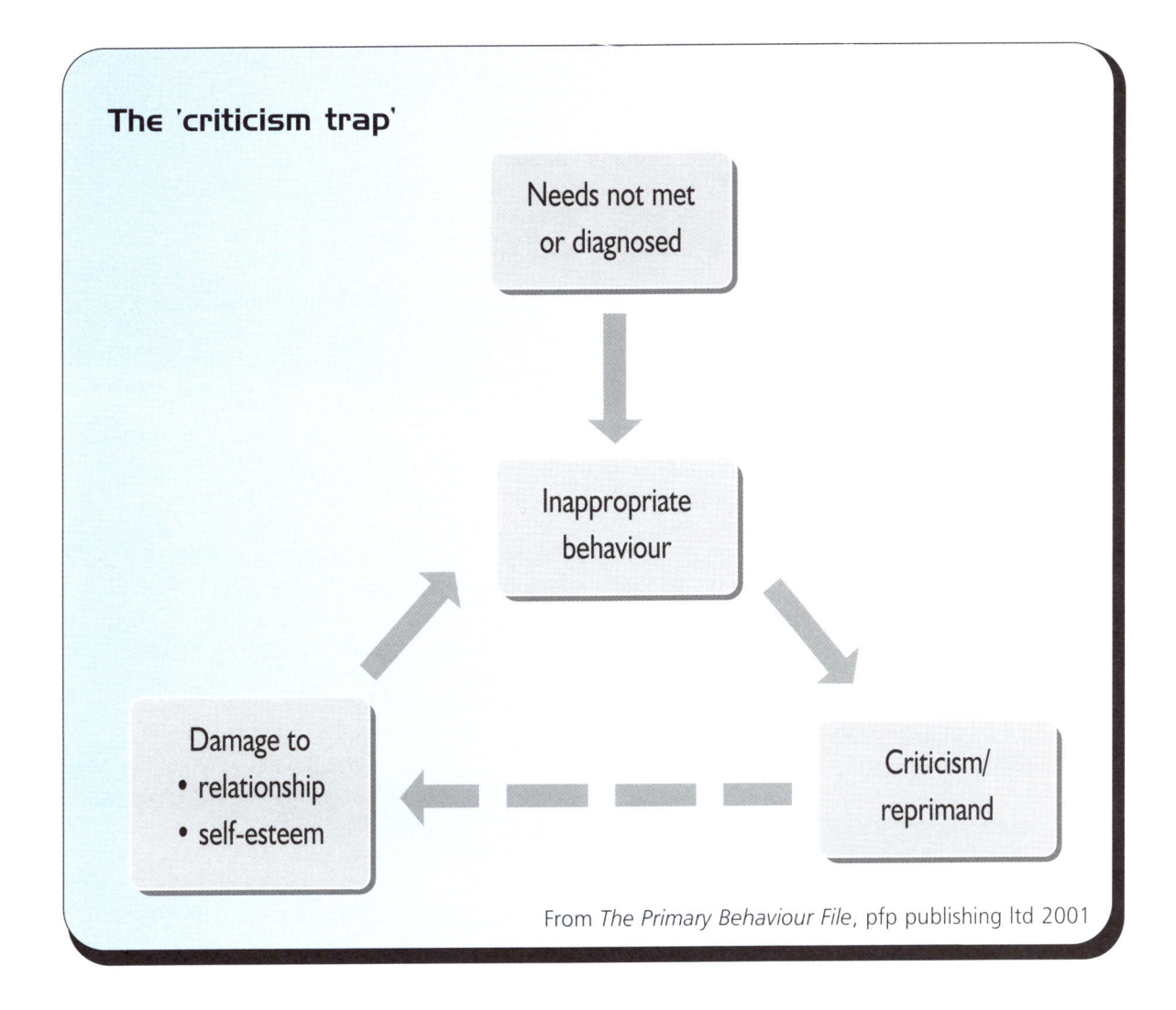

```
           Needs not met
           or diagnosed
                │
                ▼
           Inappropriate
            behaviour
           ↗           ↘
   Damage to           Criticism/
   • relationship  ←   reprimand
   • self-esteem
```

From *The Primary Behaviour File*, pfp publishing ltd 2001

child begins to lose hope in the relationship he has with the class teacher and/or his peers, many problems will follow.

Teachers must at all times be critically aware of the dangers of falling into a cycle of criticism with a difficult child. Low self-esteem often leads to poor behaviour, which may lead to criticism that reinforces the low self-esteem. This cycle must not be allowed to develop.

Expectations

It is vital that teachers have high expectations of all areas of children's work in school – behaviour, attitudes and academic work.

The most damaging attitude when working towards improving behaviour in school is that of teachers not believing that children can change and lowering their expectations accordingly – the 'What can you expect from this type of child?' syndrome. Fight it at every opportunity.

This is not asking teachers to naively ignore the very real challenges presented, but to accept that their professional role requires them to change their teaching and management approaches to help develop the attitudes, skills and knowledge that the children need to learn. With different children, this will inevitably call for different priorities. A key misconception is to interpret having high expectations as meaning that you are 'assuming that children will behave'. Many teachers then feel frustrated when they don't. The expectation of high standards needs constant scaffolding from the teacher by

- pre-empting and preventing poor behaviour by organising and managing children in a way that gives them the chance to demonstrate what they can do
- providing the role model children need
- reinforcing and encouraging the desired standards
- making children feel good about being the way the teacher is encouraging them to be.

References

Gordon, R (2001), *The Primary Behaviour File (2nd edition)*. London: pfp publishing.

SECTION FOUR

Involving and supporting parents

The children who are already exhibiting positive behaviour in our classrooms probably live in homes where they are shown love and respect. Their parents probably create firm boundaries within which the child can feel free to express himself and he is able to push those boundaries at times, knowing that his parents will be constant and reasonable in their response.

Earlier sections of this book have looked at ways in which we can conduct ourselves and at how we can create an atmosphere of calm control, fairness and justice. We have examined ways in which we can reward the children and involve them more. In this section we will look at how we can have some influence on what happens at home.

There is advice on how to involve the parents in their child's education, to help them see their child's achievements. There are ideas for influencing the way in which they speak to their child and how they can react to his efforts in positive and encouraging ways. The chapters 'Writing to parents', 'Parents' evenings' and 'Writing reports' deal with ways in which you can make contact with the parents, and how you can use these opportunities to demonstrate encouragement, promote positive views and give criticism in constructive ways. The 'When parents help in your classroom' chapter gives advice on working with parents when they come into your classroom or go on trips as volunteer helpers.

Another option is to organise workshops for parents on issues which affect their relationships with their child. The practical decisions for this will be for your school's senior management team to make – the time of day, the place, the availability of creche facilities, who will pay for refreshments and so on. The final chapter in this handbook includes ideas for workshops and advice on the content of any sessions you are able to arrange for your parents. There is a list of other professionals you could invite along and some broad ideas for the contributions they could make. There is also some detailed planning for workshops you can carry out.

Writing to parents

Making contact with the parents of the children in your class is one way of building bridges between home and school. It is a way to show the parents that you recognise and value their support, and for them to feel that they have an important contribution to make to their child's educational progress. It allows you to form a non-threatening relationship, which is a useful basis to have if any difficult situations arise during the school year. When parents know that you'll be keeping them informed about what's happening to their child in school, they won't worry as much. They can come to parents' evenings with a shrewd idea of what you will want to talk about with them. They can open the end-of-year report without feeling anxious about what it might contain.

Keep in touch with your parents as often as you can without overloading yourself even further. If you teach younger children, the chances are that you will see many of the parents every day. You can keep them informed about what is happening on a regular, informal basis. If you have something sensitive to discuss with them, phone them up or drop them a line – you can't be sure who is listening in if you talk in the classroom, cloakroom or playground at the end of the day. If the children arrive at school by bus or taxi or they're brought by grandparents or childminders, then you need to make direct contact with the parents. Don't rely on a third party to pass on your messages. The sense may be lost or they may be genuinely misinterpreted because questions cannot be asked immediately.

When you write letters to parents there are two things for you to think about.

- The style and presentation of the letter.
- The content of the letter.

You may be writing to just one of your parents on an issue that affects her or her child. You may be writing a letter which is going to be copied to all members of your class. It may be a sensitive issue or simply some information about the visit you will be making to the museum next week. Not all the advice which follows relates to every letter you will write over the space of the school year, but it is worth thinking about all the issues raised and how they will affect the particular letter you are about to write.

Style and presentation

Postcards

A quick note to say well done can be written on a postcard. Keep a selection in your room.

Use school letterhead

If you want to include personal or sensitive information you will need to write a letter that can go into a sealed envelope. Always use paper with the school letterhead. It sends a message that the content is important and that the recipient is important. Paper torn from an A4 block, or grabbed from the drawer in the classroom, says that the letter has been dashed off, written in haste or at the last moment. It looks as if you haven't thought about what you are writing. This is a real danger – you may write something quickly and then regret it later on.

Keep a copy

Keep a copy of what you have written so that you can confirm what you wrote in the event of disagreement or misunderstanding. It is also evidence that you made contact with the parent on that particular issue.

Use an envelope

Again this gives stature to the letter and lets the parent know that it contains important information.

Use a word-processor

This avoids any misreading, or potential criticism of your handwriting, grammar or spelling! It also means that it is easy to keep a copy. Set up a file for letters or save them to disk so that they can't be accessed by an unauthorised person.

The Positive Behaviour Handbook

Content

Check that you have the correct name of the parent

The school secretary will be able to provide you with this information. It starts things off negatively if the parent's name is incorrect or misspelt or she is given the wrong title.

Use the language of support

As you write, you will be giving the parent messages about your attitude to the child through your response to his work or behaviour. You will also be giving the parents a model for how they could approach or respond to their child. Use language of support and concern, not of retribution. Describe any problem in factual terms without emotive descriptions – 'I am concerned about his behaviour on the playground and want to find out what is causing it', not 'I need to speak to you about his dreadful behaviour on the playground, which won't be tolerated any longer'.

Point out the child's strengths

The way that you speak about the child can reinforce the parent's own negative or positive views of their child. If they see their child as always in trouble or never behaving and you write to tell them that there has been trouble in the class, they will immediately assume it is their child. Use as many opportunities as possible to speak well of the child, particularly if you know that this is a particular parent's view of her own child. Point out the child's strengths. Let the parent see that there is good in this child, so that she can gradually start to see it for herself and begin to respond to him in more positive ways.

Don't include confidential or sensitive information

Don't write down anything that could be interpreted as being personal, confidential or sensitive. Remember, the letter may be picked up and read by another person. There may be information which is upsetting to the recipient. If you need to speak about such a matter write to say that you would like an opportunity to talk with her about her child's 'behaviour' or 'attitude' or some other non-threatening, non-intrusive word.

Keep the content simple and factual

It's not a literary masterpiece. Its purpose is to tell the parent something that she needs or wants to know. At the same time avoid being cold or dictatorial. That approach has no place in the primary classroom and certainly won't help to build bridges between home and school.

Asking for a reply

If you need a reply, by letter, phone or in person, make that clear at the end of the letter.

Bear in mind that not all of your parents may be literate

Some may have problems with reading, others may have a limited vocabulary. To avoid embarrassment, keep the letter short and to the point, and use a simple grammatical structure. Don't use educational jargon or abbreviations. Write dates, times and places in bold print so that they can be picked out from the rest of the letter.

Translations

If English is not the parents' home language you may need to use a translation or there may be another parent who regularly translates for them. In these circumstances you should be extra careful about what goes into the letter when dealing with sensitive issues.

When might you write to parents?

All parents

There are various occasions when you might write to all parents.

Outlining expectations

At the start of the school year, you might like to explain to parents what you expect of the children in terms of effort and behaviour. Include a set of the golden rules that you have agreed with the children. If you have agreed any sanctions for those who don't stick to the rules, or any rewards for compliance, tell the parents about them. Ask the parents for their support in maintaining this code of behaviour.

Termly updates

To update them at the end of each term or the beginning of the new term, and to review the rules and how well, in general, the children are keeping them. Is there a problem with one rule? For example, if you have agreed that the children would always have their PE kit in school on the right days, but there is a constant problem of children failing to do this, you may want to draw the parents' attention to it. You can ask for their support to make a concerted effort next term to get this right.

Particular behaviour problems

If there is a serious problem with some behaviour which is affecting the class and which won't wait

> Don't write down anything that could be interpreted as being personal, confidential or sensitive

for your regular letter, you may feel that it is necessary to write to all the parents. Let them know what is going on and inform them about any actions you have taken already and the results. Tell them what you plan to do next, and of any ways in which they can help you. Make it clear at the top of the letter, or in the way that you begin, that this is an open letter to all parents – 'Dear parents of children in class X'.

Praise

To let them know that the class has behaved well. Give them examples of what you mean by this. Explain what was happening before, how you have tackled the problem and what is happening now.

Special events

To give details about a visit, a visitor, a special day, an invitation to a performance and so on.

Individual parents

There will also be reasons to write to individual parents.

Concerns about attitude, behaviour or work

If you are concerned about a child's attitude, behaviour or work, state the area of your concern and ask the parent to get in touch with you to arrange a convenient time to meet. Let her know approximately how long you expect the meeting to last, and say whether you think the child should be present, or know about the meeting. Be as positive as you can so that you don't alarm the parent or cause her to start quizzing the child – 'What have you been doing?' or punishing him – 'I've got to give up my time to go and see your teacher'.

Praise and progress

If you have been setting a child some targets for his behaviour or his attitude and effort, and they have worked well, you should keep the parents informed about any progress so that they know that things are improving in school.

Sample letters

At the start of the school year

Netherwell C of E Primary
28 Mornington Park, Alltown,
Leics.

Dear Parents,

My name is ... and I will be teaching your child this year. I am keen for him to enjoy his time in this class, taking part in the many activities I've planned.

I have talked with all of the children about how I expect them to behave and work. Together we have written a code of conduct for our room. We have called it 'Our Golden Rules'. There is a copy with this letter so that you know what we are working towards.

We have agreed that if anyone breaks one of our rules there will be some form of punishment. The first time, I will remind them of what they ought to be doing. The second time, and if they continue to go against that rule, ... will happen. If the children keep to the rules they can gain rewards in the form of ... at the end of each week.

I shall write to you again at the end of the term to let you know how things are going.

Just to remind you – indoor PE is on Mondays and Fridays and we have outdoor games on Wednesdays. As one of our rules is about always having all our equipment available in school, would you please remind your child to bring his or her things on those days!

I wish to keep you involved in your child's education as much as I can. There are the usual parents' meetings where we can look at his progress and discuss his new targets. In addition, I like to keep in touch with all parents, hopefully with good news, but if necessary to let you know of any difficulties. So don't be anxious if your child brings home a letter from me occasionally.

Over the year there will be times when I would appreciate some extra help in the classroom – when we have a practical activity such as cooking or planting seeds, or if we go on any visits. If you would like to be considered for this let me know what sort of things you'd be happy to do and any times that are suitable for you. I'm sorry, but you won't be able to bring any of your other children in with you on these occasions.

I'm also attaching a copy of our work plan for this half-term so that you know what's going on in the class and so that you can offer additional help to your child. You may be going to the library and could borrow some books on ..., or you may have some interesting items, books or pictures about ... at home that you could talk about with your child. We do appreciate all the help and encouragement that you have given your child in the past.

Many thanks for all the support I know you'll give in the coming year. I look forward to teaching your child and working with you.

Mr CE Ramsay

At the end of term

Dear Parents,

You'll be pleased to know that we've had a very good term. The golden rules are working well and most of the children keep most of the rules most of the time. We're still struggling to have the PE kit in on the right day regularly. Could you give your child a bit of a reminder about this? Thank you.

Because they've done so well, the children are going to watch the video of ... on Wednesday afternoon, and there's another small surprise for them, which they can tell you about when they get home.

Have a good holiday and I look forward to seeing you again in January.

When there's a problem in the class

Dear Parents,

I'm sorry that I have to write to you today. As you will be aware, there is a craze at the moment for collecting … cards. We let the children bring them into school on condition that they only have them out at playtime.

Unfortunately two things have happened. One is that someone has taken one child's set of 45 cards from his bag. The other is that some children are exchanging cards or playing with them during lessons.

Today I have talked to the children about honesty and about keeping hobbies for playtimes and concentrating on work in lesson times. It would be a great help if you could speak about this at home as well, just to reinforce the message. Thank you.

If this behaviour continues next week then I am going to ban … cards altogether. But I hope that the children will show that they can respect the rules and so be able to continue with the fun side of collecting these cards in school.

Thank you for your support.

When there's a problem with one child

Dear Mr and Mrs …,

I have noticed a change in …'s behaviour over the last couple of weeks. The cheerful boy we are used to has been replaced by a very quiet, sometimes moody boy. It would be helpful if we could get together to talk about what we think might have caused this and see how we can help him to overcome any worry or problem he may have.

Would you please call in, or phone school, and arrange a time when we can meet for about half an hour?

Kind regards,

When you want to tell a parent how well their child is doing

Dear Mr and Mrs …,

I thought you'd like to know how well … has been working. He has been concentrating on his work and getting it finished on time. He seems to be very happy in class now and is generally helpful and polite.

Thank you for all the support and encouragement you have been giving him.

To sum up

Don't forget to write occasionally to the parents of children who always behave well – those children who always work hard and never make a fuss. There is often limited contact with the parents of these children, possibly only a casual 'good morning' and the formal situations of parents' evenings. This can mean that you miss out on opportunities for building relationships between home and school. It is important that these children's contribution to the success of your class is recognised and that they and their parents also feel valued by you.

Parents' evenings

How can you use the opportunities afforded by parents' evenings to promote positive behaviour in your classroom? Your overall aim is to give the children a sense of self-worth, so that they don't need to gain attention in antisocial ways. You are also looking to encourage those children who behave well and work hard, and who are setting the standards you hope the others will aspire to.

Parents' evenings are the formal occasions for getting together with the parents to look at the child's progress so far, address any concerns that you or the parents might have, and plan the targets for the next stage. They are also a wonderful opportunity to develop a partnership with the parents. You can help them to go back home feeling proud of their child and what he has achieved, proud of the contribution that they are making to that achievement, and with some strategies to help them to deal with their child in ways that will continue to boost his self-esteem.

Nevertheless, for some parents these evenings can be daunting experiences. Consider the parents of your children. Some may not speak English well, or at all. Some may not have had a good experience of education themselves and feel intimidated by the occasion. Others will think they know everything there is to know about education because they have read the newspapers. Any of these can reduce the effectiveness of the occasion. Parents may arrive tense and defensive. They may come across as aggressive, when really they are insecure and trying to find a way to cope.

What can you do to calm parents' anxieties?

Make contact beforehand

If you have had contact with parents through chatting after school, or by writing to them, you will have already prepared them for this formal setting. They will have some idea of what you are going to say to them, they will make a contribution because they will have considered things you've talked about, and they will know you as a person, not just a name. They can come to the meeting with a sense of partnership.

Create the right atmosphere

You have to see parents in your classroom, so think about the seating arrangements. You are used to sitting on small chairs, but parents can find this difficult. They may have medical conditions or be overweight and find using a child's chair an embarrassment. Set up a table with some adult sized chairs in part of your room. Have any books and records to hand. If parents are to feel confident in your abilities, you must show them that you are organised and in control.

Make them feel at ease

Welcome parents in with a smile and a handshake, and show them where to sit. Thank them for coming. Explain what you will be talking about and that you welcome their comments, contributions and queries.

How can you raise sensitive issues at parents' evenings?

The formal parents' evening is not the best time to deal with sensitive issues. It certainly shouldn't be your first choice, but it may be your only contact time with some parents and you may have to broach a difficult subject with them. Only do so if you are sure that you can't be overheard by other parents.

If this is unavoidable, because these particular parents have not responded to letters you have sent, tell them that there is something which you need to discuss with them when others are not around. Then make an appointment for them to come to see you after school in the next day or two.

If parents start to tell you something which you realise is going to take some time to deal with, listen to the basic facts, explain that there isn't enough time this evening, or that they can be overheard, and then suggest a further appointment when you can all give the matter more time and focus.

If you have to deal with these matters at the parents' evening you should

- state the problem as you see it, giving examples, but not naming other children

- ask the parents if they know anything about it, the child's feelings, or any possible causes

- explain what you can do to help the situation or to correct the child's behaviour in school

- suggest things that the parents might do to tackle the problem at home, aiming for a balance between punishment for any wrongdoing and support for the child to help him learn how to behave or respond in more appropriate ways.

Ways to start the discussion

- 'I've noticed that B seems unhappy when he comes into school. Have you noticed it? Do you know of anything that is upsetting him?'

- 'B told me that he doesn't like playtime. Has he mentioned this to you? Has he given you any reasons why he feels like this? Is there anything you would like me to do about it?'

- 'I thought it might help B if …'

- 'There have been a couple of occasions recently when B has been unkind to others on the playground. It's mainly to two of the girls. Do you know anything about it?'

- 'I think we could help him to cope with this problem if we were to work together on this. If we do … in school, would you be able to do … at home to back it up?'

- 'Is there any way in which we could help you to handle him at home? Would you like to talk to the school nurse or doctor?'

This is an opportunity to offer parents advice on how to handle their child's behaviour appropriately. You can offer the following sorts of suggestions about sanctions which don't include physical punishment, and rewards that don't involve spending pounds at the local electrical store.

- Removing the television or computer from the child's room for one night. If the behaviour is repeated remove it for two nights, and so on.

- Each night for a week give the child some routine household task which has to be completed before he can go out to play with his friends.

- If he is making a fuss about wanting some expensive trainers, say that he has to earn them by, for example, washing up every night. Every task done earns him one pound towards the cost of his trainers. A compromise would be to make him earn the difference between the price they are normally prepared to pay for trainers and the cost of the particular ones he 'needs'.

- Use reward charts (left) made up of little steps, for which he gets some penny sweets, leading to a more substantial reward for completion of the whole chart. This could be a family trip to a fast-food outlet, choosing what you have for tea on Saturday, or renting a favourite video.

To sum up

The parents' evening should be the formal part of the relationship you are creating with the parents of the children in your class. It should be seen as only a part of this process, when you get together to summarise the child's achievements and plan the next steps in learning, and in behaviour and social development.

Try to use it as an opportunity to reinforce your message of partnership, as you work together with the parents to give value to each child. You have to be honest in your assessment of the child's work and effort, but aim to balance what you say so that the parents go home feeling positive about their child.

Writing reports

Your school will have an agreed format for report writing. You may have the freedom to phrase comments yourself or you may be constrained by computer-generated statements. The focus for your reports at different times of the year will be set down. As you read the advice that follows remember to use it within the guidelines agreed by the head, the senior management team and the governors of your school.

There are legal requirements about what should be included in the child's end-of-year report, but essentially the purpose of the report is to sum up the child's achievements throughout the year. It is an opportunity to

- summarise the child's learning in every subject taught in your class
- comment on his effort and the progress he has made
- report on his behaviour in class and on the playground, his relationships with other children and with adults
- suggest ways to continue the progress or to address areas of difficulty in learning, effort or behaviour
- elicit the support of the parents where this is appropriate.

Write it in a positive way

This doesn't mean glossing over the bad points or ignoring them altogether. It's about recognising effort and achievement. These may not be in direct proportion to each other. Some children will work consistently well to achieve quite low results in terms of grades or levels. Others can put in little effort and end the year with higher levels. Some schools have report formats which allow you to grade effort as well as achievement, and these figures can make an informative profile of the child in class.

When parents read the report they should see a rounded picture, 'warts and all', of their child. Include those areas where the child should be making more effort, or where he could achieve a higher level if he applied himself more to the task in hand instead of talking to those around him. Parents need to know this. It needs to be recorded in the report so that his next teacher will be able to spot when he makes a real effort to address his behaviour or put more effort into his work, and for her to be able to comment and praise him for this.

There shouldn't be any shocks for the parents in the report

If you have been keeping in touch with them throughout the year the parents will know of your concerns and will know that you have been trying to sort things out with them and the child. They will recognise what you have to say. It is simply a summing up of all that has happened and a statement of where the child is now.

They should feel a sense of pride in their child's achievements

It can help the parents to see all that their child has achieved throughout the year, and to know that they helped to get him there.

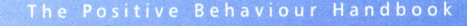

Include the child

Use the second person as you write.

> 'You have worked hard in this term to improve your imaginative story writing. You have produced some excellent work as a result of the concentration you have been giving to these lessons, and the extra reading you have done at home. Well done.'

If you write to the child rather than about the child it fosters a sense of pride and it makes the report a more personal document. Writing it this way makes you think about what messages you want to give the child about his work or behaviour. Imagine you are saying it to him personally. Phrase it so that he will understand. Make clear the cause and effect of either working hard or not doing so.

Looking forward is essential

Both the child and the parents need to know where he should be going next and some strategies he may need to apply if he is to do this. You can include some broad targets, either to point to the next step of learning or to provide some ideas for addressing problems.

> 'Now that you have shown how able you are at creating interesting stories, it would be worth trying to develop your use of interesting vocabulary. One way you could do this is to read more books by different authors. This will give you fresh ideas to use in your own writing.'

> 'You have been using some superb words and phrases in your stories to make them more interesting to the reader. I'm pleased that you are doing this despite the fact that you sometimes struggle with the spelling. If you are able to use a computer over the holiday, you could write some stories using a programme that will show you when you have got a spelling wrong. Use a dictionary to put these right. If you keep getting the same word wrong, spend some time rewriting it to try to learn it by heart.'

Include comments from the child and the parents if possible

If you can include comments from the child and the parents, the complete document will give the whole picture. You can read the report with the child and encourage him to respond and either write his own comment or have someone scribe it for him. You should make sure that you listen to the child's evaluation of his achievements. Does he value what he has achieved? Is he disappointed in his work? Does he know when he has done well, or does he make unfair comparisons with others? You might ask the child to write comments about his progress over the year in key areas and include this as part of the report that goes home (below). See the chapter 'Developing high self-esteem and learning about criticism' for more ideas you could use for this.

Some schools have space at the end of the report for parents to add their own comments when they have read the report. For younger children who are not yet able to complete a format such as the one below, the section for the parents to fill in could include space for 'things he likes to do outside of school' and so on. It gives the message that everyone's opinion is worth having and worth recording for the future.

To sum up

Use the opportunity of reports to reinforce the message that everyone can do something well. Hopefully the children and the parents will accept your honest appraisal of achievements, of progress made and of effort and behaviour which have contributed to the wellbeing of the group. You can demonstrate to parents how to speak to children in positive ways, that you can phrase a message, even a critical one, in a way that spurs a child on to greater things, and that we don't need to be harsh or condemnatory to get our point across.

Think about the whole of this school year as you write about each of these.	
What I have learned	
How I have tried during lessons	
My behaviour during breaks and lunchtimes	
Clubs I have joined in school	
Things I like to do outside of school	

When parents help in your classroom

Apart from the practical support you and the children are getting, try to think of this as an opportunity for you to demonstrate to the parents different ways of dealing with children. You can show them how adults can

- speak to children in supportive, non-critical ways
- praise children without being patronising
- respond to inappropriate behaviour
- encourage appropriate behaviour and responses.

Just like the children, the adults who come into your room will be picking up signals from you, they will be learning by watching and mimicking your behaviour and your responses to the children. You can actively encourage them to do this by inviting them to watch you as you respond to the children and to follow the lead you give them.

Speak to children in supportive, non-critical ways

- *'Try one more on your own and then I'll come over and help you with the next one'* to encourage the reluctant worker.

- *'I've put a line under the words where you need to check your spellings. Use a dictionary and see how many of them you can do on your own'* to encourage a poor speller.

- *'If there isn't a tick next to your sum it means you need to think about it again'* means that there isn't a page full of crosses and the child can have a second chance to do well.

- *'Work with your partner to jot down some of your ideas. The one who can write the quickest, do the writing. The other one will be expected to tell us the ideas you both came up with when we get back together in five minutes'* allows children to use their strengths and work cooperatively.

Praise children without being patronising

- *'That was a really good idea, Sam.'* Everyone can make a contribution and no matter how small it may be it needs to be recognised.

- *'I do like the way you've used the white paint to make that part shine out.'* Let the children know exactly what it is that they have done well. Be precise in your comments.

Respond to inappropriate behaviour

- *'Mrs ... could you sit next to ... and help him put all those pieces back in the box?'* You are handing over responsibility to another adult to make sure that the mistake or act of defiance is put right, and you can continue to focus on the rest of the class who are getting on with what they are supposed to be doing.

- *'Sam, please move away from ... so that he doesn't disturb you with his chatting.'* You are again giving attention to the child who is behaving appropriately, recognising that he is uncomfortable and allowing him to remove himself from this situation. This is a skill which children and adults can usefully employ in many situations. At the same time you are isolating the child who is behaving inappropriately, and you are letting all the children know that this behaviour won't be tolerated.

Encourage appropriate behaviour and responses

- *'Thank you for picking that up.'* By noticing positive behaviour and giving public recognition to it, you are reinforcing the standards you want to see in your classroom. The child can feel a sense of pride, is the centre of attention for a moment and then life carries on.

- *'It's good to see everyone at this table ready, with your books open.'* Let the children know that they have done something commendable, even if it is a routine that you would expect in your classroom. It gives messages to others, who will try to do the same themselves.

- *'I can see seven, eight children sitting with their arms folded and looking to the front.'* When you ask the children to sit together for a story, the plenary session of the literacy hour or whatever, some will make an additional effort. Spot it and comment on it so that everyone is aware of it, and those who tried will be glad that they did. Younger children will usually respond to this by

> By noticing positive behaviour and giving public recognition to it, you are reinforcing the standards you want to see in your classroom

joining in with the named action and the counting.

If a parent is helping in your room she needs clear guidelines

- Tell her exactly who will be in her group. It is best to avoid giving her children who you know are fairly likely to misbehave. If anyone will need additional support, for example, in reading instructions, point this out beforehand. Tell the parent what to do, how much help to give and any additional learning support or aids the child will require.

- Give her a detailed list of tasks to be done, how long each one should take and when you will want the class back together again.

- Provide a list of useful questions that she can ask to get the children thinking, and vocabulary that you want the children to use.

- Talk about the level of noise that would be acceptable for this activity and what you will expect her to do if it gets too loud.

- Talk about the need for children to stay on task, and not to be wandering about the room. Make sure that all the equipment she will need is ready and that she knows whether she or the children will be tidying it away and when they should do this.

- Remind her that you will be maintaining overall control of the children in the class and that she should only intervene with her identified group of children.

Tell her what to do if she has any problems with the children's behaviour

A simple three-point approach is enough for most parents to cope with.

- Ask the child quietly and calmly to sit down/speak quietly/share equipment.

- Repeat the request in a firm voice, but without shouting.

- Send one of the other children to ask the teacher to intervene.

You can then repeat the request, and if necessary remove the child in question to do something less exciting. The children will soon learn that this is what will happen and that they will lose the chance to work with an adult helper.

You are giving the parent a chance to practise ways of handling her own child at home. She sees that you don't need to shout and scream, that you can retain your dignity. The child learns a lesson on cause and effect – messing about and ignoring a polite request means that you lose out on a treat that you can see others are enjoying. You may be able to talk to the child about this and then let him join in the next group to do this activity, in this session or next week. This can give the parent confidence – she can see that the strategy works, that the child has learned the lesson and that she has managed a difficult situation and maintained her self-respect.

She also needs to know what rewards she can give

Younger children in particular see the giver of rewards as someone with power. Give the parent some small stickers to reward any child who is working well, quiet, polite, who finishes his work in the given time, who helps to tidy up and so on. The little sticky-backed dots that you can buy in most stationers are cheap and effective for occasions such as this.

Remind her that she should give the children lots of verbal praise and encouragement. It might be appropriate to let her see a list of the kinds of things you would say to the children, as shown above. Encourage her to tell the children why she thinks something is good, and whether she approves of their behaviour, their effort or the work they are producing. Remind her to be fair and to try to praise each child for something during the session.

To sum up

When you have parents in your room, use the opportunity to do two things.

- To demonstrate how to handle children so that they feel encouraged and valued. Even if children are misbehaving you should show how to remain in charge of the situation, keep your cool and never belittle or undermine the children in any way.

- To enable the parent to try out some of these approaches in a situation where there is a backup – you – if she fails to maintain control, and where the children are less likely than her own children to answer back or be rude.

Parents will take home some of these skills and their own children will benefit from a more reasoned response to their behaviour.

Parent workshops

When children are small, parents can rely on the health visitor for advice and support as they learn to be good parents. Once the children start school, the school medical services take over the care of their health. Personal contact is more difficult because of the number of children in the care of school nurses, and the fact that they may work from a centre at some distance from the home. Parents can feel isolated as they struggle to deal with aspects of their child's emotional and social health. Schools are there to educate the children, but they can also play a part in influencing the quality of the parenting they receive at home. When parents and school tackle any problems together there is a much greater chance of success. Organising workshops for the parents can be a positive way to address some of the issues that may surface in your school.

Why 'workshops'?

This word gives the message that it is going to involve everyone. It's not going to be some professional talking at the parents. You don't have to be clever and able to learn something. Instead, you have to be willing to have a go, to try something out, to share your experiences to help other parents who are just beginning to face a difficulty that you have overcome. They are practical and will help parents to gain some new skills.

Organisation

If you know your parents well, you may already know what time of day suits them best. If not, send out a simple questionnaire. You need to consider the following.

- What space is available in school?
- Can this space be used during the day, straight after school, in the evening?
- Are the providers you are hoping to attract able to work in the evenings?
- Will you need to provide creche facilities? Where? Who will run it?
- Will you provide refreshments and will they be free of charge, or at a nominal charge?
- Who will chair the meetings?
- How long should each meeting last?
- Who will pay for any expenses incurred?
- How often should the workshops be held?
- Will you have to limit the number of participants because of available space?

INVOLVING AND SUPPORTING PARENTS

The Positive Behaviour Handbook

67

Other professionals

There are professionals in the health service who would be able to present some of the workshops if you give sufficient notice. You will need to let them know all the practical details of when and where, but it is also worth preparing a document which states your aims in running these sessions, and a summary of what you would like them to cover. It may be possible to organise a planning meeting for all those interested in using this as a forum for contacting parents, and plan the programme together.

Ideas for a programme aimed at promoting positive behaviour through the raising of children's self-esteem, ways to cope with your children's behaviour and support their emotional development are shown in this box.

SCHOOL NURSE	Transition issues Bedtime routines
PRIMARY MENTAL HEALTH WORKER	Emotional development Understanding the 'inner child' School phobias Boundary-setting
SCHOOL DOCTOR	How illness can affect mood
EDUCATIONAL PSYCHOLOGIST	Behaviour management programmes
EDUCATION WELFARE OFFICER	Truanting issues – keeping your child in school

Each of these professionals will have other areas which they could talk to parents about, but you need to make sure that the subject matter meets your stated objectives.

Using the expertise you have in school

Theoretically, any member of the school staff could run a workshop for parents, but there are steps your headteacher can take to make this an integral part of the school's plans for improvement, rather than leaving it as an afterthought, tacked on to the end of a busy schedule. If it is to work it must be thoroughly planned.

Long-term planning at a management level

The headteacher will need to discuss the idea with the governors and senior management team first. It will be time-consuming to organise and run, and therefore there must be a clear focus on what you hope it will achieve. You could include it as part of your School Improvement Plan, in a section about behaviour, or as part of a focus on community work.

The aims of your school will form part of the school's prospectus. They can be included in the home–school agreements. The objectives to achieve or maintain those aims could be written into the SIP. They may include something similar to this.

Aims
- That all pupils should be able to work and play in a safe, caring and supportive environment.
- That all staff should be able to work in a safe, caring and supportive environment.

Objective
To increase the children's self-esteem in order to reduce antisocial behaviour in the classroom and on the playground.

Targets to meet the objective
- Introduce sanctions to respond to name-calling, calling out, talking during lessons and so on.
- Introduce rewards for appropriate behaviours by all children.
- Use class rules to set boundaries for children.
- Provide training for lunchtime staff.
- Improve contact with parents about children's work and behaviour.

Steps to meet the targets
- Each class teacher to write to parents at the start of each term.
- Each class teacher to write to individual parents with praise or concerns about children's work or behaviour as necessary.
- Parents to be invited to help out in school.
- End-of-year reports to include comments by children and parents.
- Headteacher to organise a series of workshops to help parents promote their child's positive behaviour.

Planning with the staff

You will have to discuss the programme as a staff, looking at the whole picture as shown in the SIP, and identifying what you want to get out of this part of it.

Staff who are keen to take part in presenting workshops should be encouraged to do so. If any training is needed then you can do this as a whole-school twilight session, bringing in some outside help, or you may be able to use the skills of members of your staff.

All staff can take part in the planning and preparation of the workshops. It's important that everyone knows and agrees with the messages being given to the parents. It also helps individual members of staff to deal with parental enquiries or feedback.

What can staff offer?

Staff may have particular expertise in, for example, behaviour management or child development, that they can usefully share with the parents. Others can use their educational expertise.

- *Subject coordinators* – to deal with aspects of the children's learning that might be new to the parents or have changed in some substantial way, in order that parents can help children with their homework or understand what their child is talking about when he explains something that he's been doing in school.
- *Early years teachers* – to look at the importance of play in children's development.

What are we trying to achieve through these workshops?

You need to work out exactly what message you want the parents to get from the workshops you run. Essentially they will gain some practical skills which they can use in their interactions with their own child. These skills and ideas are the sugar coating to the pill. There will be some hidden messages that you need to know, but that they don't need made explicit.

Handling the child with confidence

When the parents know what they are doing, why they are reading with their child, where this fits in with the child's broader education, this gives them confidence. Then the parent can act with the assured authority of someone who knows, rather than the aggressive authority of someone who is trying to make the child think that she knows.

If she doesn't know an answer she will have strategies to deal with this. If she knows most things then she can own up to not knowing this one thing. She knows that she can find out, she knows that she has the support of the school.

She also knows that other parents don't always know the answers, that everyone struggles with something and that this doesn't diminish you as a person.

Dealing with difficult situations

By giving parents a range of strategies to try out, they can feel less threatened when things don't go exactly to plan, or when they can't provide the ideal circumstances for their child. They will hear other parents who are experiencing similar situations, they can discuss things that work or offer advice to other parents.

They can find out that it is okay to give up when you can't solve something amicably, to avoid confrontation and bad feelings. They can find out that there is a support system out there, staff in school, other parents, other professional support and advice, that they are not alone.

Showing respect and expecting respect

Parents can learn skills which enable them to speak to their children, to listen to their children, and not just to react to them with negative words and shouting or aggression. They can learn what they should expect of their children, ways to occupy them and how to defuse situations.

All of these will help in avoiding the potentially negative situations that result in arguments. Children will start to feel valued by their parents, and recognise that their parents have done something for them so that they can enjoy their time at home.

Ideas for workshops

All the ideas here aim to provide parents with information and expertise to help them in their interactions with their own children. As they learn how to react in positive and calm ways to their children, they will be able to support and build on the work you are doing in school to promote positive behaviour through the development of children's levels of self-esteem.

Each session can be led by a member of the school's staff and should last about 45 minutes.

Start each session with a welcome. Introduce yourself and outline of the aim of the session.

> Parents can learn skills which enable them to speak to their children, to listen to their children, and not just to react to them with negative words and shouting or aggression

Workshop 1

HELPING WITH HOMEWORK

You will need

The OHTs 1, 2 and 3 provided on pages 71-73.

Copies of the handout provided on page 74 to give to parents at the end of the workshop.

Introduction 5–10 minutes

Getting children to do their homework can be a time of conflict in many homes. Why?

- Children refuse to come and start.
- Children argue with the parents when they try to help them.
- Children get frustrated because they 'can't do' the piece of work.
- Older children interfere with younger ones because they think they know it all.
- Younger children, especially pre-schoolers, tear paper, scribble on books and annoy older children.

Brainstorm

Brainstorm with the parents what other difficulties they encounter. Make a list of the problems on a flipchart.

Realising that others have problems with homework can make some parents feel better, knowing that they are not alone.

Main activity 20–25 minutes

Some things you can do to ease the tension and make this an enjoyable time for all members of the house.

Use the three OHTs provided. Show one at a time, talking through each of the points in turn, discussing it with the parents, encouraging them to give their opinions about which are good ideas and which are asking for trouble. Explain each good point a little more. Don't simply read out your list.

OHT 1 – HELPING WITH HOMEWORK – WHEN

When to do it

- Just as the children settle down to their favourite television programme?
- As they arrive home from school?
- When they've had their tea?
- While you're cooking?
- After they've gone upstairs to bed?
- As soon as they get up in the morning?
- While they're eating their breakfast?

The important facts

- Children need a break and a run around when they get home from school. They may be hungry and need to eat before they can concentrate. No one can do his best if he's tired or hungry – his mind will be on other things.

- Children won't concentrate if they feel they're being deprived of something such as a favourite television programme or a game of football with everyone else.

Some strategies you could try

You could get together with the parents of your child's best friends and agree to a time for homework that everyone sticks to. If your child is a loner, agree a regular homework time with him and stick to it.

OHT 2 – HELPING WITH HOMEWORK – WHERE

Where to do it

- Downstairs near the television?
- In her own room?
- On the floor?
- At a table?
- Near their computer?

The important facts

- Children need a defined space, away from other children. They should have room to lay out all the things they may need to use – pencils, rulers, a dictionary, books. If you have more than one child needing to do homework they may be able to share a space and work at opposite ends of the same table. If they are likely to argue or annoy each other, they should work one at a time.

- Children need to have the fewest possible distractions. Television screens draw the eye and the children's attention. Some music playing will be less distracting and many children can work well with this.

Some strategies you could try

- Allocate the table in the dining room or kitchen for homework at times when you don't need it.

- Provide a small table in your child's bedroom if she has her own room or she shares with a child of a similar age who is also doing homework.

- Keep younger children out of the area while your child is doing their homework. Let her see that you are giving her status, that her time to do her work is important and that you respect her need for peace and quiet.

- If she has to work in the same room as the television, turn it off or keep the volume down low.

OHT 3 – HELPING WITH HOMEWORK – DO I HELP?

Should I help him?

- Always, sometimes, never?
- Show him how you used to do it when you were at school, even if the teacher has shown him a different way to do it?
- If he gets something wrong, shout at him?
- Find him some books you have, to help him find out some answers?
- Give him the right answers to put in if he's struggling?
- Go with him to the library after school the next day, to get some useful books?
- Help him to find a suitable site on the Internet to help him with some information he needs?

The important facts

- Children need your support and encouragement. Use expressions like 'have another go at that one', 'think again', 'are you sure?' rather than scolding. It makes a better experience for you both, and your child will feel really good about himself when he spots his mistake and puts it right.

- If your child's work is always correct because you are giving him the answers, the teacher won't realise that he is struggling with that level of work. She may even give him harder work, thinking that he has understood. If he has needed a lot of help, write this on the end of the piece of work or call in and have a word with the teacher. Try to tell her what it was that was giving him particular trouble – spelling, subtraction, and so on. Your child will see that you are on his side, and that it is okay to admit that you don't understand and would like a little more help. There is no shame attached to not understanding something.

Some strategies you could try

- Look through the homework with him and see what books or equipment he needs. If he needs additional books or information, put off doing the work until you have managed to gather all the resources together. You may need to go to the library to borrow books or use the Internet facilities there. If there is something, perhaps a dictionary, that you don't have at home, ask the teacher if it's possible to borrow one. Now let him get on with the work.

- If he needs help, be positive, show him where to look or how to start, and then let him try for himself.

- If you don't know how to do something, tell him the truth. Ask the teacher if she can tell you how to do long multiplication or whatever is causing the problem. If a number of parents have problems with the same thing she may be able to give you a 10-minute session after school one day.

- If neither of you can do something, and you've had a genuine attempt at it, write a note to the teacher, or speak to her, explaining the problem.

The Positive Behaviour Handbook

Handout – Helping with homework

When?

- When she's had a little break, but before she gets tired.

- Avoid times that clash with her favourite television programme.

- You could get together with the parents of her best friends and agree to a time for homework that everyone sticks to. If she's a loner or doesn't usually see her friends after school, agree a regular homework time with your child and stick to it.

Where?

- Allocate the table in the dining room or kitchen for homework at times when you don't need it.

- Provide a small table in your child's bedroom if he has his own room or shares with a child of a similar age who is also doing homework.

- Keep younger children out of the area while your child is doing his homework. Let him see that you are giving him status, that his time to do his work is important and that you respect his need for peace and quiet.

- If he has to work in the same room as the television, turn it off, or keep the volume down low.

Do I help?

- Look through the homework with her. See what books or equipment she needs. If she needs additional books or information, put off doing the work until you have managed to gather all the resources together. You may need to go to the library to borrow books or use the Internet facilities there. If there is something, perhaps a dictionary, that you don't have at home, ask the teacher if it's possible to borrow one. Now let her get on with the work.

- If she needs help, be positive, show her where to look or how to start, and then let her try for herself.

- If you don't know how to do something, tell her the truth. Ask the teacher if he can tell you how to do long multiplication or whatever is causing the problem. If a number of parents have problems with the same thing he may be able to give you a 10-minute session after school one day.

- If neither of you can do something, and you've had a genuine attempt at it, write a note to the teacher, or speak to him, explaining the problem.

- Use phrases to encourage her – 'have another go', 'think about that one again', 'are you sure?'. Don't scold her. If you feel yourself getting cross or annoyed, walk away and let her get on with the work by herself.

Workshop 2
HEARING YOUR CHILD READ

This workshop should be held after the 'Helping with homework' workshop, so that you have already talked with the parents about the general issues connected with getting the child to do work at home.

You will need

Video clips of you, or another teacher in the school, reading with individual children. If you can set up a video camera on a tripod this can be left running while you go through your usual routines, and you can then edit the film to leave only the parts that are relevant. *Make sure that you have written permission from the parents of any child you involve.* Try to read with several children at different stages of reading development. Choose children whose reading development is average for their age, to avoid any unkind comments or comparisons. Using your own staff and children helps parents feel that this is what is right and acceptable in their school and for their children, and not something which has come from some higher authority.

You will also need copies of the handout provided on p78.

Introduction 5–10 minutes

Summarise where hearing the child read fits in with all other aspects of teaching a child to read.

- Whole-class teaching of reading strategies.
- Group teaching of reading strategies and word recognition.
- Individual teaching of strategies and word recognition.
- Opportunities throughout the day to revise word recognition or to practise reading strategies.

Activity 1 20 minutes

What do teachers do in school that you can do at home?

Talk about each of these stages, showing short clips from the video to illustrate each of the points you are trying to make. Each clip should last no more than one minute.

Choose the right book

Make sure that the book is at the right level for what the school wants the child to do. When working with the teacher for group work, the book will be challenging to the child. This lets the teacher introduce new things that she wants the children to learn. When the child brings a book home it will be at a comfortable level, so that the child can practise what he has been learning, and he can show you what he can do. The teacher will know what book the child has, and that it is at the right level for the task ahead.

Choose the right place

Sit in a suitable place so that you and the child are comfortable and can see the book clearly. *(Show an appropriate part of your video.)* The book will be in front of the child, with the teacher looking over. The light will be on the page, not in the child's eyes. They will sit slightly apart from others who may distract the child's concentration, and away from noise which might prevent the teacher from hearing what the child is saying, and vice versa. You can choose a place that is away from the television, is cosy and comfortable, but well lit. If you are sitting on a sofa, let the child hold the book and you look over. Make it a special time, for both of you, with no interruptions if possible.

Talk about the book

Talk about the whole book with the child. Together, read the title, identify the author (the child may not be able to read these as names often have complicated spelling patterns or be from a different language), discuss the picture and try to guess what the book will be about. *(Show an appropriate part of your video.)* From Year 2, the children should also be reading the blurb on the back cover, or on the inside page, to find out more about the book. This helps the child to realise that covers give a lot of information which will help them to choose a suitable book for themselves. You can also talk about whether the book is fiction (made up) or non-fiction (facts) and how you can find this out from the front cover (the title and the pictures will usually give this away).

Use the pictures

Use the pictures to help with additional information not written into the text. Early books rely heavily on the pictures for this. There is a lot of detail to be picked up from the pictures. 'Look at Bunny's face. Why do you think he is smiling?' 'Have you noticed the old fox hiding in the hedge? What might he be thinking?' At the next stage the pictures can give details about things that are not in the text, but which the reader needs to know if he is to make sense of the story. 'Look at all the traffic; what a busy street that is. Now we know why Bill's mum said that he was never to go to his gran's on his own – he would have to cross that road!' It is only at a much later stage that the child can pick up all of the hints and clues in the text and enjoy a story through his own imagination.

Start to read the text

Young children may need to be reminded about

- text/picture differences.
- top to bottom.
- left to right.

The teacher will point to the words as she reads them in the early stages. When the child is starting to join in and take over the reading, he will be expected to point to the words. This helps to keep his eyes focused on the right place. *(Show an appropriate part of your video.)* Older children reading a page with lots of text on it may appreciate using a bookmark under the line. This can be any piece of paper or card, shaped like a ruler.

Talk about the words

Talk about the way that the writer uses particular words. You may comment on interesting words or phrases – 'her tears splashed down', 'the car went roaring down the road'. If there are any unusual words, try to work out what they mean by thinking about the context in which they're being used. If you're not sure about them look them up in a dictionary. Ask the child if he knows what a word means if you think he may not have met it before.

Talk about the story

Talking to the child about the story or the information in the book is a check to find out if the child is actually 'listening' to the words as he reads. For young children retelling the story shows this. Can he put the main events in the right order? *(Show an appropriate part of your video.)* Part way through you can ask the child if he can work out how the story will end. 'Do you think she'll get home safely?' 'Do you think the writer can twist things around so that the astronaut eventually reaches Mars?' At the end of the reading, ask the child's opinion about the story. 'Did you like it?' 'What was your favourite part/character?' 'If you'd written the story would you have made that dog chase the rabbit or would you have let the rabbit get through into the garden?' 'What difference would it have made if the main character had been a boy instead of a girl?'

Activity 2 15 minutes

What to do if he is struggling or is a reluctant reader at home

For younger readers, read the book to them first. Go through the book looking at pictures and trying to work out what the story is going to be about. *(Show an appropriate part of your video.)* Then read the words to find out if you were right.

For older children who are starting to tackle whole pages without any pictures, read a page or a paragraph yourself first. Then read it with the child, speaking together. Then let the child read it on his own.

An older child can 'practise' a page or more first. He can sit on his own, working through the text and asking you for help with words which are giving him a problem. When he is ready he can read it to you.

Read alternate paragraphs with your child. This is good if your child is determined to read a book which is actually too hard but which he is keen to read. Films such as *The Lord of the Rings* may encourage your child to tackle *The Hobbit* or even start on *The Lord of the Rings* books themselves.

Alternative strategies

If you are having real problems getting your child to read at all, don't make it a battleground. Try some of these alternatives.

You read to him

Children who hear stories can use the words and ideas to help them become better writers. Children who hear stories usually want to go on and read for themselves eventually. You can read more complex stories that he will enjoy but that are too hard for him to read on his own at the moment.

Read to him and leave him the book

You read to him and then leave him on his own with the book so that he can look through it for himself. Try leaving it by the bed, so that he can read it when you're not looking. That way, he won't lose face, but you will in fact have won – just don't tell him this!

Ask him to read to a younger child

Ask him to read a baby book to a toddler to help you out. This can increase his confidence in that he can do something that the younger child can't do, that he is reading something that you were prepared to read, that reading something simple doesn't mean that you couldn't read something harder 'if you wanted to'.

Give him something other than a book to read

Try some reading material that isn't a book – instruction sheets for games or models, recipes, television programme details, maps and routes for your holiday, the guidebook from the visit you made last weekend, the write-up for a film you might go and see and so on. Comics need reading. Magazines and so on form the bulk of our everyday adult reading, not 'hard' books!

Reluctant but able readers

Add interest to the activity

Able readers sometimes don't like reading out loud. How would you feel if I asked you to read out loud to me now? Even though you could do it, it might be an uncomfortable experience. It slows down the pace of reading, and children can feel frustrated by this. Ask your child to read the next chapter of his book and then choose one part of it, between a half and one page long (probably about a hundred words – this is the amount used to test the children at Key Stage 1), to read out loud to you. It might be a part he thinks you will like, or his favourite part, the funniest bit or whatever. Or you could point out a piece of similar length and ask him to prepare it, to check that he knows all the words, to think about expression, to add voices for different characters that would appeal to him. Remember, he must enjoy this activity – it's not meant to be a punishment! Then he can read it out to you.

Misreading words

When listening to able readers remember that it is common for them to 'misread' words. They may change the order of the words to fit in with their own speech patterns. When the children were small and you had to read the same book over and over, you would occasionally do this and your child will have complained and told you to read it properly. It's a sign of a good reader, and you don't need to comment on it.

If all this fails...

If he still won't read at home, leave it for a few weeks. Let the teacher know that he isn't reading with you. She may be able to arrange for him to read with a volunteer who comes into school, or she may be able to offer you some other strategies suited to your child's particular difficulties.

Parents' own reading problems

If you're not a confident reader yourself, you may have some anxieties, which the child will pick up from you. While your child is reading the early books this may not be a problem, but it could cause some difficulties when he starts to read books which are a challenge to you. You can still do some of the activities we've been talking about.

If you let the teacher know, she can make sure that your child has read the book at least once before he brings it home, so that your role will be to encourage and praise him, not to read to him. You can borrow stories on tape, so that you can listen to them together as you follow the print. You can also use computer programmes that highlight the words as they are spoken.

You can watch a film or television programme together, and then talk about the way the creator got the message across, about the good and bad characters, about the story, whether you liked it or not, what was good about it, what worked well. You can encourage a young child to retell the story so that he practises putting events in order, and summing up the main points.

In summary 5 minutes

Talk about how often children should read at home, and for how long. Remind parents that this is not to replace bedtime stories or the reading children will do on their own from library books or their own collection.

Handout – Encouraging your child to read

Ten top tips

1. Set aside a special time and place to read with your child.
2. Share a book every day.
3. Read to your child as well as listening to your child reading to you.
4. Encourage your child to 'have a go' at new words and praise his efforts.
5. Read a wide range of books and comics.
6. Use the whole book, including the cover and the pictures as you read.
7. Talk about the books and your personal preferences.
8. Provide a special place for your child to keep his books, whether they are on loan from the library or ones he owns.
9. Join the local library or make use of the school library. Books are expensive and this gives your child access to a wide variety at no cost.
10. Have fun – use different voices and accents, read some funny stories and poems, laugh together at comical illustrations.

The Positive Behaviour Handbook

Workshop 3

Fun for free

Ideas for wet days and half-terms for young children.

Dressing-up clothes 15 minutes

These can open up a world of fantasy and imagination. They will encourage a child's story-telling abilities. They allow children to become someone else. The timid child can be brave and strong. The quiet child can be a roaring lion. The worried child can act out his concerns. Everyone can have fun.

Look through your own wardrobe, or in charity shops and jumble sales for potential dressing-up clothes. Don't go to the expense of shop-bought clothes. These tend to limit the child to being a super-hero, with a fixed character and expected story line.

Have a selection of prepared clothes and potential clothes for them to look through for ideas.

- Flowing nightdresses in fine fabrics, net curtains, evening dresses (princesses and queens).
- Curtains, skirts or the skirt of long dresses with waistband and fastenings removed and ironed smooth (capes).
- Waistcoats or the tops of the dresses with the sleeves, collars and fastenings cut off to resemble waistcoats (cowboys, princes).
- Cut the ends from the waistbands of long, full skirts, and thread a length of elastic through, tying the ends firmly. Even young children can then dress and undress themselves.
- Anything glitzy and glamorous will appeal to little girls. Scarves and oddments of shimmery fabrics, hats and fake fur can make them feel very special.
- You can add beads and sequins to otherwise dull fabrics with fabric glue.
- Have a box of 'jewels' for them to add to the effect. Charity shops and jumble sales are your best source of old-fashioned strings of cheap beads.
- Shoes and boots can give the finishing touches. A simple rule about not going up or down the stairs wearing these is a good idea.

Remind parents about small items and the dangers these pose for young children. Children should be reminded about safety, or the parents should avoid these items if there are pre-schoolers at home.

You might want to suggest that the parents come together on another occasion to make over some items. They could all look around for potential fabrics and clothes and bring them into school one afternoon and transform them. Large cardboard boxes or plastic crates can be used for storage.

If boxes are used the parents can decorate them as another wet day activity at home with their children.

Castles and cars 15 minutes

If you can provide some large boxes you can set them up as each of these things in turn to demonstrate their flexibility. You could even take them into the classroom earlier, challenge the children to turn them into as many different scenarios as they can, and photograph their results. Show these to the parents and then brainstorm other ideas.

Empty cardboard boxes are freely available. Supermarkets always have some around. You may be lucky enough to have a very big box from a furniture delivery. Ask around your local shops.

Stacking boxes up to make walls, using them as if they were bricks, makes a safe and flexible construction. It can be run into on your bike without hurting you, just like stuntmen do.

The wall might surround a castle. Draw and cut out some arched windows from paper and stick them onto your castle wall.

Use a number of boxes to make a play kitchen. Draw, cut out and stick on paper doors for the washer, gas rings or electric plates for cookers, and dials and knobs wherever they are needed. Or you can use marker pens and draw them straight onto the boxes. Stand a plastic washing-up bowl on the top of one box to make a sink.

A small box can be a cot or a bed for the dolls to use.

A huge box may be big enough to let a child sit inside. Then it can be a car or a chariot, a ship or an aeroplane. Improvise steering devices for these from paper plates stuck on the ends of short lengths of broom handle. Draw and cut out dials and headlights. Use kitchen foil if you want it to look like chrome or steel.

A green towel or old curtain draped on the floor can be an island to which your boat can sail. A shiny piece of fabric can be a new planet you discover while out in your rocket.

If you can't get hold of boxes, drape a blanket over the space between two kitchen chairs to make a den. Or drape it over your folding clothes drier. Children love secret places where they can 'hide'. Put some cushions inside, or let them have a picnic lunch in there. It can become an army tent, a bear's den, a cave or a secret hide-away for bandits.

To sum up 5 minutes

Start the children off, giving them a few ideas to get them going, and then let them use their imaginations. Play with them if they want you to join in, trying to enter their world of imagination. Have fun with them for a limited time, and then say a firm 'Now I've got to do … and you can carry on playing without me.'

Discover the Primary Leadership Collection

Primary Leadership Books

Primary Leadership No 46 Finance
ISBN 1 874050 66 X
£15.00

Primary Leadership No 47 School Improvement Planning
ISBN 1 874050 67 8
£15.00

Primary Leadership No 48 Environmental Issues
ISBN 1 874050 68 6
£15.00

Each book comes with a CD-Rom

Primary School Handbooks

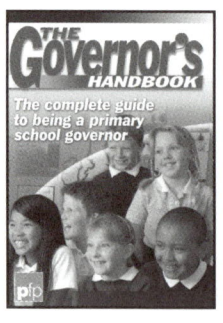

The Governor's Handbook
The complete guide for the school governor.
ISBN 1 874050 54 6
£15.00
Additional copies £7.50

The Positive Behaviour Handbook
The complete guide for headteachers and staff for promoting positive behaviour throughout your school.
ISBN 1 874050 71 6
£15.00
Additional copies £7.50

The Governor's Handbook comes with a CD-Rom

The Solutions Series

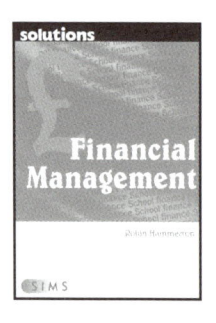

Raising Additional Income
ISBN 1 874050 72 4
£5.00

Your Budget
ISBN 1 874050 73 2
£5.00

Financial Management
ISBN 1 874050 74 0
£5.00

In association with www.sims.co.uk

Online Training

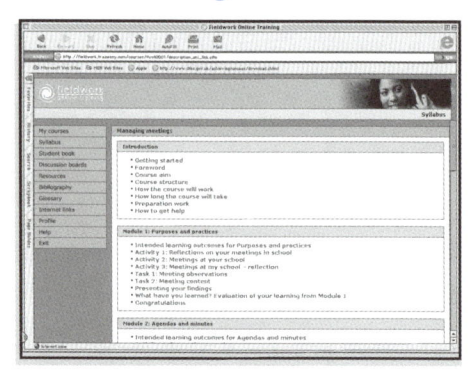

Two courses currently available

Managing School Finance
£60.00

School Self Evaluation for Governors
£60.00

Order Now
T: 0845 602 4337 F: 0845 602 4338
www.pfp-publishing.com

practical resources for school leadership

pfp